DEER &
DEER HUNTING'S®
GUIDE TO
HUNTING
THE
RUT

Published by

Krause Publications a division of F+W, A Content + eCommerce Company
700 East State Street • Iola, WI 54990-0001
715-445-2214 • 888-457-2873
www.krausebooks.com

To order books or other products call toll-free 1-800-258-0929
or visit us online at www.shopdeerhunting.com

ISBN-13: 978-1-4402-4325-7
ISBN-10: 1-4402-4325-5

Cover Design by Dave Hauser
Designed by Sandi Carpenter
Edited by Chris Berens

Photography by Dustin Reid

Printed in the United States of America

contents

INTRODUCTION

DANIEL E. SCHMIDT, EDITOR-IN-CHIEF OF DEER & DEER HUNTING

The ways we approach deer hunting sure have changed over the past 20 years. What was once an activity limited to a few days each November has turned into a year-round obsession for many hunters. We plant food plots, run trail cameras and hunt with bows, crossbows, rifles, shotguns, muzzleloaders and handguns.

One thing that will never change about the hunt is our fascination with the whitetail rut. This frenzied two-week portion of the season is what we all live for each year. It's that one magical time when mature bucks are most visible and that one time when we all have an equal opportunity to bring home the deer of a lifetime.

What you're holding is *Deer & Deer Hunting's* finest collection of rut-hunting articles ever assembled in one work. It might only be 128 pages long, but this book includes decades of insights into the whitetail rut; why deer behave as they do during the breeding season; and how to hunt it most effectively.

The roster of contributors is a virtual who's-who list of North America's best whitetail minds and rut hunters.

You'll learn more about deer biology and how it relates to the rut from such authorities as John Ozoga and Jeremy Flinn. You'll also learn Charles Alsheimer's insights into deer behavior that will help you better understand how, when and where to place your treestands.

After learning the hows and whys of rutting behavior, use the tactics of top hunters like Patrick Meitin, Bill Vaznis, John Eberhart and more to get the drop on the buck of your dreams.

Enjoy this book. It is the result of nearly 40 years of work from America's first and foremost whitetail hunting authority: *Deer & Deer Hunting* and the Stump Sitters Whitetail Study Group.

SECTION 1: PRE-RUT

chapter 1

GET TO KNOW THE PRE-RUT BUCK

CHARLES J. ALSHEIMER

▶ MORE THAN 20 YEARS AGO, this magazine invited its field editors on an early October deer hunt and brainstorming session in northern Wisconsin. For three days, fellow field editors Kent Horner, Richard P. Smith, Larry Weishuhn and I hunted and swapped knowledge about whitetails with the *Deer & Deer Hunting* staff.

The crew predicted hunting whitetails in early October would not be good. They were right. Few of us saw deer and no one killed a buck. But the whitetail discussions during our cabin time more than made up for the lack of deer sightings.

Naturally, the topic of hunting pre-rut bucks dominated the conversations — particularly as it related to why we weren't seeing deer. The consensus was that what is often referred to as the October lull, was one of the toughest times to hunt whitetails. Although I felt quite knowledgeable about deer behavior back then, in truth, I knew very little compared to today.

Since then, I've received quite a whitetail education. The years that followed provided many hunts to some of the best whitetail haunts in North America. As eye opening as those experiences were, there were two other things that provided a greater education — year round deer photography and raising whitetails for behavioral study.

Hunting, photography and raising whitetails has allowed me to literally live with deer 24/7, 365 days a year. It's been an incredible experience that's given me insight into the world of the whitetail I never could have found by merely hunting them.

SEASONAL BEHAVIOR

Many deer behaviors are common, regardless of the season. However, much of what they do is seasonal. Consequently, the way whitetails act and react during September and October is much different than during the rut.

Whitetails have gained the reputations of being very secretive creatures, especially mature bucks during September and October. As a result hunters often refer to this time as the September lull, October lull or pre-rut lull, because of the lack of deer sightings. However, we must remember that the deer do not make such classifications. No one thing causes them to be secretive. Rather, the lack of deer sightings is a result of a host of factors.

PHYSICAL CHANGE

Daylight begins to decline rapidly by the end of August, and the nights become cooler. The shorter photoperiod causes a whitetail's winter fur to replace its summer fur by mid-September.

Although the fur is not as thick as it will be by November, it can be a real liability for whitetails because of the warm daytime temperatures that are common in early autumn. If daytime temperatures are normal or above normal, deer sightings will be scarce during this time because deer do not have sweat glands to cool their bodies. They have to rely on their mouth and ears to cool down, and neither works particularly well.

FOOD IS THEIR ADDICTION

Have you ever thought about what you'd feel like if you were to eat a four course Thanksgiving meal with all the trimmings for two straight months?

My guess is that you'd not only feel miserable but you would look like a blimp at the end of the 60 days. Well, that's what a whitetail goes through from the end of August to the end of October.

The amount of food whitetails can consume over this period never ceases to amaze me. It's like they have an inner voice telling them that they need to eat, and they can really pack the food away.

During most of the year, deer will typically forage for food every four hours, if they are not pressured by man. However, during September and October their feeding schedule increases, particularly at night. Each deer is different, but generally during this time they'll attempt to feed every two to three hours — sometimes more often. If not threatened, each feeding session will last up to a half hour. It's not uncommon for a whitetail to consume more than 12 pounds of food in a single day.

The amount of weight whitetails put on during the pre-rut will depend on their metabolism. However, my research deer typically exhibit a 20 percent increase in body weight from August to the end of October. This weight gain, coupled with having a winter fur coat is a major contributor to their lethargic nature prior to the rut.

HUMAN ACTIVITY

A whitetail's daytime activity during the pre-rut is driven by two factors, temperature and predators. As previously mentioned normal or above normal temperatures can cause whitetails to shut down. They simply cannot function properly in heat, no matter how hungry they are.

But as bad as heat can be at suppressing deer activity, the presence of humans can be far worse. It doesn't seem to matter whether the human presence is in the form of farm activity or people physically intruding on deer territory.

The lunar research that Vermont whitetail biologist Wayne Laroche and I have been conducting the past 16 years has revealed much about deer activity. Unlike the hot-to-trot rut, when buck activity is high during the two hours either side of daylight, our cameras have told a much different story during the pre-rut.

During September and October, more than 80 percent of daytime deer activity occurs in the last hour of daylight. Unlike the rut, where there can be great deer activity in the hour or two after sunrise, very few deer are moving around at dawn in early fall, unless it's unseasonably cool. Even then, it is pretty much over within the first hour of sun up.

Research has shown that it doesn't take much to turn whitetails nocturnal. When a whitetail knows what its predators smell like, look like, and sound like, it will never forget those lessons for the rest of its life.

Sure, trail cameras are one of the greatest scouting tools developed in the last 50 years, but they are often overused by hunters. If hunters truly realized how incredible a whitetail's memory is I believe they'd think twice about traipsing all over their hunting area to retrieve photos from their cameras.

Few hunters realize that the warm moist temperatures of early fall cause their scent to linger longer, which tips deer off to their presence. It is paramount that hunters keep their on-the-ground and trail camera scouting to a minimum in areas they intend to hunt.

BEDDING BEHAVIOR

Thick hair, warm temperatures, full stomachs, and human pressure are the primary things that ground whitetails during the pre-rut. It's only when temperatures cool and the presence of predators subsides that deer have any desire to move about and search for food during daylight hours.

I've studied whitetail bedding behavior extensively. Except for during the dead of winter, when conditions are severe, there are few times of the year that can match early autumn for the amount of time whitetails spend in their beds. About the only things that will cause them to move around during daylight hours are insects and predators.

From sunup to an hour or so before sundown whitetails will typically stay in the same bed for two to four hours before getting up, stretching and moving a few yards to relieve themselves.

Then, they'll often re-bed in the same bed or a location within yards of where they were bedded.

While bedded, they chew their cud, groom themselves and sleep in various positions. It's only when they sense daylight fading or the temperature dropping that they'll begin getting on their feet to search for food.

LITTLE SEX DRIVE

Bucks spend most of their August days in bachelor groups that were formed in spring or early summer. Research has shown that a buck's serum testosterone and testicular volume levels in early September are half of what they are in early November, when each peaks. Because of this, these bucks show little interest in does throughout September and early October.

About the only time a buck will interact with does during this time is when it finds itself at the same food source as the does.

I've always found it interesting the way bucks seem to totally ignore does when they feed together in early autumn. Instead, bucks seem more inclined to feed, groom and bed with the bucks that make up their bachelor group. In many ways this lack of sex drive is nature's way of keeping bucks stress free in the months leading up to the rut.

As each September day inches toward October, a buck's testosterone level begins to rise. With it comes an increase in rutting behavior. One of the first behaviors to ramp up is friendly dominance matches between bucks within a bachelor group.

Commonly known as sparring, bucks engage in antler to antler shoving matches as a way of determining pecking order within the group. For the most part sparring matches last less than five minutes and only rarely become violent.

Other ways bucks determine hierarchy during the pre-rut is by displaying their attitude through stare downs and threat walks, with their ears pulled back and hair bristled. Although comical to observe, each is a very effective non-combative way for bucks to sort out who is boss.

Bucks also broadcast their presence to deer in their home range through scraping and rubbing behavior. Bucks and does are able to recognize each deer by the scent they leave on rubs and scrapes as well as from the tracks they make because each deer has a unique odor. Both scraping and rubbing behavior begins slowly after velvet peel. As a buck's testosterone levels rise rubbing and scraping increase greatly by the time late October arrives — before peaking when the breeding phase of the rut starts in November.

CONCLUSION

There is no doubt that daytime deer sightings in September and October are hard to come by because of low sex-drive, human pressure, warm temperatures and an overabundance of food. All contribute to why many deer hunters believe the pre-rut is the most difficult time to hunt.

But, the deer haven't left the woods. In fact, understanding the causes of the lull can help you also understand when and where to hunt mature bucks during this difficult period. ■

chapter 2

THEY CALL MY LAND HOME

JEREMY FLINN

▶ DEER HUNTERS AND MANAGERS ACROSS the country read articles and books, watch television shows, and attend outdoor conventions in an effort to improve their local deer herd and ultimately, their hunting. One of the most discussed topics is how to keep mature bucks on their property throughout the year but particularly during hunting season. From many years of research, we now know that unless you install a high fence that is nearly impossible.

Whether you have 50 acres or 5,000 acres, because of the size and irregular shape of a mature buck's home range (especially during the hunting season) a buck's movements will not be captured entirely within the property's boundaries. But don't get discouraged. Think about it ... a single hunter can't cover the entire home range of a mature buck anyway. Sure, we all want to protect them as much as possible, but that's why many of us hunt "fair chase;" sometimes we get them and sometimes someone else does.

Regardless, it's hard to cover that much ground and therefore we will likely miss many opportunities. But what if you could focus your efforts on an area typically eight to 10 times smaller than the buck's entire home range, and know that this is where he spends at least 50 percent of his time? Sounds too good to be true, but this is his core area. So while it may not be practical to keep a mature buck entirely on your 100 to 200 acres, it is absolutely feasible to have him spend the majority of his time on your land. Even better yet, it is even realistic to have multiple mature bucks' core areas on your property. Enough talk. Let's see how you can make this happen on your piece of deer dirt when it counts — during hunting season.

1. DON'T OVERTHINK IT

Food. Water. Cover. Does. If you provide it, they will come! It seems like a no-brainer, but far too often deer hunters overemphasize one of these factors while

neglecting the others. Typically the food factor is the main one overemphasized. In today's deer community, a guy's 50-acre property will have numerous acres in food plots! Although food plots are a great management tool, they work just as well in moderation.

If you have hunted long enough around food plots, you know that as soon as acorns start falling deer lay off the plots. It's not uncommon to see multiple mature bucks feeding in a food plot or crop field in summer, but as hunting season approaches and bachelor groups break up, it becomes more of a rarity. However, by having adequate food available on a property, multiple mature bucks are able to coexist often without encountering each other.

During all seasons, a buck's core area will almost always include a stable food source whether that is a food plot, agriculture field, or productive acorn flat. Focus on creating food sources that provide year-round nutrition. This may be in the form of perennial food plot or native browse, or a strategic rotation of annual plots. The longer a food source is available, the more dependent and comfortable a mature buck becomes feeding on it. If you have ever watched a mature buck pick up acorns through an old oak flat versus eating at a pile of shelled corn with no fields within a half-mile, you know exactly what I mean.

Water is a factor that varies much more than food. In most regions of the whitetail's range, deer will achieve the majority of their daily water intake through food consumption. I'm in no way saying deer don't drink, but their water supply for survival is typically extracted from plants they eat. However, in arid regions and during droughts or warm spells, water is very important. It is likely that mature bucks in arid or drought-affected regions will have a water supply of some sort in or very near their core area. If you think water is a critical factor in your area, make sure you at least target it in the early hunting season when temperatures are the warmest.

2. IMPROVE THE KEY INGREDIENT

Cover is probably the most neglected of the four factors. It is not uncommon in many areas to hear "cover is not a limiting factor." There may be enough cover to survive, but we are talking about having the cover that mature bucks desire. There is a big difference between the two.

With its natural camouflage, almost anywhere a whitetail goes it can have cover to hide. However, mature buck cover provides enough security to allow him to get to be older. In my personal experience as a biologist and hunter, mature buck cover is typically some of the thickest, most impenetrable areas that are not influenced by humans. In the Southeast, that may be a 3- to 5-year old clearcut; in the Northeast, it may be a thick conifer stand. It is almost impossible in today's world not to mention the monster backyard bucks many of us encounter. Many times this isn't the thickest of cover or undisturbed by humans, but it is typically free of one thing: hunting.

With only soccer moms in SUVs as a harvest threat, many bucks in these areas will become mature no matter the cover. So what if your property lacks mature buck cover? Create some! The easiest way is to open up the canopy through tree cutting. Leave the tops of the trees and the light penetration over time will sprout new growth. It is also a good idea to stay out of this area by identifying it as a sanctuary (we will discuss this later).

The doe factor is a little harder to control. The more attractive you make a property to mature bucks, the more does that are likely to congregate. The theory that more does means more bucks in the rut can lead to a lot of frustration. With more does on a property during the rut, the less time a mature buck has to work to find a mate. This usually leads to bucks being less mobile because of a less active chase phase.

Although too many does can make hunting tough, too few can be just as bad, if not worse. I always encourage every serious deer manager to conduct a trail camera survey at least every two years to determine their buck-to-doe ratio entering the hunting season. A ratio of two does to one buck will keep mature bucks' attention on the does on your property, as well as providing a relatively intense rut. Manipulating the doe population relies primarily on the amount of does you (and your neighbors) are harvesting. If you have too many does, shoot more; too few, then you may want to lay off a bit. If your neighboring properties are hammering does, then you may have to take the high road and not harvest any in order to keep that optimal buck-to-doe ratio.

3. ADDRESS PRESSURE CONCERNS

Pressure is the No. 1 killer of mature bucks on properties less than 1,000 acres. No, it isn't literally killing them, but it absolutely kills your chances to harvest one. This is an aspect of deer hunting that many either completely ignore, or are in denial that it is an issue on their property.

I'll get into details later on why you should not ignore it, but first let's address those who don't think it is a problem. First, do you hunt deer on your property? If so, perfect. You are pressuring your deer. I don't care how mindful you are about wind, what scent-elimination system you use, or if you get dropped in by helicopter. If you are hunting on your property, that is putting pressure on your deer, especially mature bucks. Now that we have identified that, as long as you are hunting this is an inevitable issue: how do we minimize the effect?

One of the easiest ways is to just stay out of certain areas on your property. Whether you call them sanctuaries or refuges, these areas are designed to provide deer security in an undisturbed setting. The area can be as little as a ½ acre or as large as 100 acres. More often it is set up to include a major bedding area that you are likely not to bother for most of the year.

If you are a deer fanatic like me, staying out of part of your property is fighting a losing battle. I often tell my clients that going in once or twice in the late winter or early spring is acceptable to look for sheds or do habitat work. Many also will do a last-effort deer drive at the end of the season. If you are doing this work to harvest more deer, I encourage you to do whatever you want! That is the beauty of it being your property. In the long run, creating a place of peace for deer will often drive multiple mature bucks onto your property, especially if your neighbors are not giving them any space.

Although I said I don't care about your wind-carefulness, scent elimination methods, and your approach to and from your spot, the truth is these are all extremely important in reducing the pressure on mature bucks. It only takes one bust to ruin a stand for the rest of the season or, even worse, run that mature buck off your property for good.

These processes are often trial and error, especially how you get to and from your spot. If you are bumping deer going into your spot each time, you need to stop! Pull up an aerial map and then create a path that avoids these areas. It may be the long way around but by not disturbing those deer you have definitely increased your chances at observing a mature buck from the stand during that hunt.

CONCLUSION

Holding a mature buck entirely on your property is not realistic for most landowners, but by taking a few extra precautions and providing everything they require you will drastically increase your chances at having multiple mature bucks call your land home. It will likely take time and patience, but the more mature bucks utilizing your property, the better the chances you have at putting another wall-hanger on the ground. ■

chapter 3

BIG BUCK SANCTUARIES

STEVE BARTYLLA

▶ ON THE SURFACE, EVERYTHING WAS against me. Illinois' second shot-gun season had just ended. The early December temperatures were in the 70s, with winds gusting to more than 30 mph. Further, the bucks were almost in hibernation, recovering from the rut. All that rarely adds up to a winning hand.

Still, family commitments left only three days for me to fill my 2012 Illinois bow tag. I had to make it work. Thankfully, Reconyx pictures revealed a good buck con-sistently hitting a clover plot at the edge of a large sanctuary.

Between the high winds and lack of stout trees, I knew I'd need a ladder stand. I'd invited *Deer & Deer Hunting's* Brad Rucks down to hunt, and although I didn't like bringing the extra bodies into my spot, I'd need the help of Brad and his cameraman, Jay Elioff, to get the 22-foot ladder up safely in those winds.

Several hours and a shower later, I was perched in the new setup. Even with the intelligence, I had doubts. In fact, I'd become convinced that I wouldn't see a deer.

Soon after that, I noticed a spike the big boy had been hanging with. Just to be safe, I got ready.

Sure enough, Mr. Big was a couple of steps behind. With more than an hour of shooting light remaining, in wretched conditions and having endured the worst the area's hunters could throw at him, the buck began feeding at my clover plot.

When he stepped into my shooting lane I was already at full draw. Checking the retina lock on my sight, I made the torque correction and sent the Rage X-treme tipped Easton flying.

As the arrow hit home, I knew the tracking job would be short and easy. The deer piled up just out of sight, less than 60 yards away. I had him tagged, gutted and in the back of my truck before the sun set.

That story was an easy choice when thinking of an anecdote illustrating the bene-fits properly planned sanctuaries deliver. Daylight buck movements during all phases

of the season, regardless of hunting pressure or weather conditions, is the goal. Will it happen every day? No, but sanctuaries can be big difference makers.

WHAT'S A SANCTUARY?

In the purest definition, sanctuaries are areas off limits to hunting and human intrusions. The only reason to enter is for recovering deer.

I have two exceptions. The first is post-season scouting and any improvement work the sanctuary requires. Both should be done many months before the season and condensed into as tight a time as practically possible.

The other is during the season. If you find an absolutely killer stand location within the sanctuary while scouting, I suggest setting it up. Then, save it as an ace in the hole. Only hunt it when the phase of the season and weather conditions are perfect. Additionally, limit hunting a sanctuary to no more than twice a season. Following those rules strikes the balance between the benefits sanctuaries can provide and maximizing hunting opportunities.

Speaking of benefits, sanctuaries attract and hold deer on your hunting grounds. It does little good to offer the best food and water and construct the perfect harvest plans if hunting pressure drives deer to neighboring properties. When done right, a sanctuary provides the illusion of safety, which holds and sucks in neighboring deer fleeing pressure.

Also, sanctuaries encourage daylight movement. Pressure, or more accurately fear, makes deer shift to being exclusively nocturnal. Simply remove the fear by giving them safe, unpressured areas to move during daylight, and daylight activity will increase. Assuming the property is hunted intelligently, that activity then spills outside of the sanctuaries.

PROPER SETUP

So, what's the proper way to set up a sanctuary? Every property is different, so a one-size-fits-all approach is ill advised. However, some general guidelines apply.

First, not all bedding areas must be sanctuaries, but all sanctuaries should contain bedding areas. Continually bumping deer out of their beds is the quickest way to drive them off a property. On most properties, strive to have at least 75 percent of bedding areas within sanctuaries.

Tough-to-hunt areas are also good candidates. If you can't safely hunt an area, you might as well let the deer have it.

On the flip side, you should rarely include primary food sources. The same goes for killer low-impact stand locations. Remember, your goal is to kill deer as much as it is to hold them or encourage daylight movement. Obviously, food sources shouldn't be overhunted, but I sure want the option of throwing a few well-timed shots at them. I also want to hunt a lot at funnels separating bedding and feeding areas.

Additionally, positioning sanctuaries on the inner portions of properties reduces losses to neighbors. When sanctuaries are established along the property lines, it increases the odds of deer crossing the fence during daylight. When sanctuaries are at the inner portions, deer must at least get through you first.

Finally, I believe few folks dedicate enough property to sanctuaries. I don't worry about their shape or number on a property. I find percentage of cover to be vastly more important. I let the lay of the land determine shapes and numbers.

In most cases, I set aside 80 percent or more of deer cover as sanctuary. I understand that's a lot, but the rewards are well worth it. Also, I can always tailor a sanctuary so it has an hour-glass border, which creates a good funnel, provided it offers safe access.

The result is concentrating the food sources and productive, low-impact hunting locations into huntable areas. At the same time, high-impact locations and most bedding areas are off limits. Consequently, the property offers good movement between the sanctuaries and hunting areas, providing great low-impact stands for hunting relaxed deer.

CONCLUSION

It's difficult to overstate the power of a sound sanctuary strategy. Through the years, hunting has trained deer to be more cautious and shift more to a nocturnal lifestyle. Sure, reversing that is easier on a 1,000-acre chunk, but my clients have success on as little as 30 acres. The results on 30 are not as dramatic, but simply getting Mr. Big out of his bed with five minutes of shooting light left can be enough. In hunting, seconds can make a tremendous difference, and sanctuaries can provide that and much more. ■

chapter 4

RESEARCH ON MOCK SCRAPES

JOHN J. OZOGA

▶ AS I DISCUSSED IN THE October 2013 *Deer & Deer Hunting* ("Pole Position: What Can we Learn From Fake Rubs"), white-tailed deer rely heavily on scent-marking at antler rubs and scrapes, commonly referred to as signposts, to communicate information of social significance, especially during the breeding season. There's good evidence deer can communicate individual identity, dominance rank, physical condition, breeding status and other bits of evidence through glandular secretion and urine deposited at rubs and scrapes.

Compared to antler rubs, however, whitetail communication via scrapes is more complicated. It's also a subject that has been elaborately abused and fictitiously presented by outdoor writers and the deer scent industry for hunting purposes.

If you follow popular literature concerning whitetail scraping behavior, you'll find mention of boundary scrapes, territorial scrapes, community scrapes, communal scrapes, hub scrapes, primary scrapes, secondary scrapes, breeding scrapes, travel-lane scrapes and more. Of course, writers seldom agree on the terms between themselves. And I seriously doubt such an elaborate array of scrape terminology is warranted.

Although we don't fully understand many aspects of whitetail signpost communication, it's my contention much can be learned by applying an artificial study approach, as demonstrated in the previous fake rub article.

Here is my experience using mock scrapes as a means of determining when, where and why scrapes are made — and who is responsible.

THE SCRAPE

When trying to unravel the mysteries of whitetail scraping behavior, I believe it's essential to stick to basics. Don't make the subject more complicated than it really is. Carefully consider the anatomy of a scrape and the physiological reasons behind scrape behavior before trying to psychoanalyze every bit of pawed turf you find. Recognize, for example, that the full scrape sequence involves scent-marking overhead limbs, pawing the ground and urinating into the pawed area. Further, these behaviors might occur independently of each other year-round.

Odor communication in deer at scrapes might involve urine, saliva, vaginal secretions, specialized skin glands and probably some other things we don't fully understand.

Secretions deposited on overhead limbs at scrapes could come from the forehead gland, preorbital gland, nasal gland or possibly saliva. Secretions in the pawed soil likely come from urine and the interdigital, metatarsal or tarsal glands.

Also, remember that a buck's scraping ability is determined by his physical, physiological and behavioral maturity. It's also affected by his reproductive condition, dominance status and probably other factors we don't know much about. Invariably, mature bucks do the best job of scraping.

If you read my previous article concerning fake rubs, you'll remember that compared to mature bucks, yearling (1½ years old) bucks commence rubbing later in the season and usually rub smaller stems but still make roughly one-half as many rubs as older bucks. When it comes to scraping behavior, yearling bucks demonstrate even less polished skills. In the absence of mature bucks, yearlings only make about 15 percent as many scrapes. Therefore, you'll find little serious scraping activity in deer populations harboring few mature bucks.

AN ARTIFICIAL STUDY APPROACH

Despite the seemingly complex nature of scraping behavior, in the mid-1980s, I concluded the most important feature of an active scrape was the overhead limb. Because a well-used scrape can be eliminated by removing the overhead limb, I theorized the opposite was also true. That is, bucks should also be induced to scrape simply by providing a properly positioned overhead limb in a favorable location.

In 1987, I set up a study within the Cusino square-mile deer enclosure to determine if white-tailed deer would make scrapes beneath human-positioned limbs. At the time, the enclosed deer population consisted of nine adult males, 26 adult females and 21 fawns.

In August, I selected 20 areas along deer trails with open understory vegetation that appeared favorable for scraping but lacked suitable overhead limbs. Two sugar maple saplings — trimmed of leaves and lateral branches — were nailed (using aluminum nails) to separate trees about 30 feet apart at each area and left in an upright position so the terminal ends were out of reach of deer. The stems varied from 4 to 8 feet long, but each was relatively slender and bowed slightly downward when suspended over the trails

On Oct. 8, the saplings were fastened so the terminal end of each centered about five feet over a deer trail. I cleared away litter from beneath one limb of each pair to expose a circular area of soil. Thus, deer were offered the overhead limb at one site and an overhead limb and exposed soil at the other.

Bucks converted 24 of the 40 artificial sites (60 percent) into scrapes from Oct. 8 through Nov. 12. They did not show preference for those with exposed soil, in terms of the proportion of test sites pawed or the frequency with which they repawed them.

That experiment demonstrated that bucks could easily be induced to scent-mark limbs and scrape where I wanted. Exposing the soil wasn't necessary. All that was necessary was to place the proper type of overhead limb in the right place.

Based on my observations, I concluded that preferred scrape sites were those with concentrated deer activity, an open understory, relatively level ground and moderately dry, easily exposed soil.

Given my success, I arbitrarily divided the enclosure into 15 compartments of roughly equal size. Within each compartment, I selected one to four favorable look-ing scrape sites that lacked overhead limbs. In all, I selected 50 sites. I then set up two sugar maple saplings about 30 feet apart at each site for future deer scraping behavior study.

These 100 limbs, distributed throughout the enclosure, served as my experimen-tal sites the next five years. The advantage of my scheme, of course, was that I not only had established areas to inspect for pawing, but I had a large number of spe-cific limb tips available to test various controlled scenarios and examine for scent-marking.

Without going into a lot of detail, here are some of things I learned about white-tail scraping behavior by using a highly artificial but scientific study approach.

YEAR-ROUND SIGNPOSTING

Although whitetails make most (if not all) antler rubs during their hard antler phase, certain aspects of scent-marking at scrapes probably occur year-round.

My studies found that deer readily scent-mark at scrapes from May through November, but that the type and intensity of marking varies seasonally. The most frequent scent-marking occurred in May and June and October and November, but the seasonal pattern of scent-marking, limb mutilation and ground pawing at scrape sites varied.

Based on breakage of the limbs or the presence of hair on the limb tips, I found that 94 percent of the test limbs were scent-marked by deer. Although deer occa-sionally ground-pawed during the spring-summer period, most such behavior did not intensify until autumn; 60 percent of the limbs were scent-marked before serious ground-pawing started.

It's interesting that I detected no serious limb-tip mutilation until October, at the same time bucks initiated serious ground-pawing. During summer (non-reproduc-tive months), deer marked overhead limbs quite gently, giving heavily used limb tips an oily or greased appearance. They treated the limbs more roughly during autumn (reproductive period), chewing the limb tips or breaking them with their antlers. Whether they urinated at these sites is not clear.

PAWED TURF

Therefore, the manner in which deer scent-mark limb tips above scrapes changes seasonally. Because bucks are more inclined to paw, urinate and tarsal-rub at scrape sites in autumn, this also hints that substances deposited and messages conveyed in such marking likely differ throughout the year. Interestingly, 50 percent to 80 percent of the observed full-fledged scrapes occurred annually during September and Octo-ber, before the first doe bred.

In 1988, I also conducted a study to determine if scent-marking during summer influenced the amount of scrape activity at a particular site during autumn. I did this by lowering one limb at each paired-limb site throughout summer while leaving the companion limb out of deer reach until autumn.

Of those limbs left down for possible summertime scent-marking, 80 percent

developed into full-fledged scrapes during autumn, compared to a 62 percent paw-ing-rate for the up-limbs. Also, deer were more than twice as likely to repaw scrapes beneath the down-limb sites.

None of my 100 test-limb sites were pawed by deer in May or June. However, deer pawed several other sites each spring and summer, indicating the full scrape sequence played a subtle but potentially important role in buck behavior even dur-ing the non-breeding period. Camera monitoring at one such site April 30 revealed a 4½-year-old buck standing on his hind legs to mark limbs more than 6 feet high. Also, fresh urine could be seen in the pawed site. About three hours later, a 2½-year-old buck inspected the site.

This suggests that some prior (summertime) scent-marking at potential scrape sites increased their autumn use. However, not all limbs marked during summer developed into scrapes in autumn. Likewise, 75 percent of those limbs that did not show obvious scent-marking during summer also became active scrapes in autumn.

MESSAGE SENDERS AND READERS

From May 1991 through February 1992, I used trail cameras to photograph deer using scrapes. I used various protocols, including random sampling of the 100 test sites and at natural scrape sites, in an attempt to identify the message senders and readers.

Results from these photographic studies confirmed my suspicions. Namely, the primary markers and readers involved in limb-marking are bucks. Of 76 deer pho-tographed marking or inspecting overhead limbs, 86 percent were bucks, 6 percent were adult does and 8 percent were fawns, despite a herd comprised of roughly 30 percent bucks, 30 percent does and 40 percent fawns.

By comparison, I photographed 89 deer at ground level in or near active scrapes during October and November. Of those photographed, 26 percent were bucks, 13 percent were adult does and 61 percent were fawns.

Bucks were photographed smelling the limb tip, some had their antlers or forehead up to the limb, and others were obviously mouthing the tip or moving it along their snout. Most of the scent-marking appeared to be by bucks 3½ years or older, especially during the breeding season. But even younger bucks marked limbs during summer.

Of 16 adult bucks in the enclosure during this series of tests, all but two were identified in photographs at limb tips overhanging active scrapes. Five bucks were photographed at one limb, and seven were recorded at another.

In other words, all deer were attracted to scrapes, but does and especially fawns paid more attention to olfactory messages deposited through urine than to glandular secretions left on overhead limbs. However, bucks were more highly attracted to limbs above scrapes.

SCENT APPLICATION

As mentioned, mimicked ground-pawing beneath artificially positioned overhead limbs did not increase deer scraping activity. So, I went further in a series of tests to determine if pawing plus application of a commercial doe-in-heat scent or buck urine enhanced their use by bucks.

Using 20 pairs of my artificially positioned limbs, beginning in early October, I applied a doe-in-heat lure beneath one limb of each pair three times a week during a three-week period. The companion limb received no special treatment. I compared weekly pawing rates beneath the treated and untreated limbs through mid-November, which covered the most active scraping period in northern Michigan.

During the test, bucks pawed 14 treated sites and 14 untreated sites. Six treated sites and seven untreated sites were repawed one or more times. In other words, I couldn't prove that treating the scrapes made them more or less attractive.

RESPONSE TO BUCK URINE

In 1988, I initiated a four-year study to evaluate the effects of buck rut urine applied to mock scrapes. My objective was to determine if I could advance the rutting behavior of bucks and, in turn, trigger earlier-than-normal breeding behavior among enclosure does.

During alternate years, I made mock scrapes beneath one limb of each pair, complete with mimicked pawing and about 2 ounces of urine collected from a prime-age buck during the rut. During treatment years, I serviced the 50 mock scrapes daily from Sept. 5 to Oct. 6, but only freshly pawed the mock scrapes twice a week from then until Nov. 7.

Deer response to the treated mock scrapes was impressive, to say the least. More than 90 percent of the treated mock scrapes were visited by deer during the first week after construction. Overall, the deer visitation rate in September was about double of that in earlier studies when I only tilled the soil beneath artificially positioned limbs.

Seasonal scraping patterns during the non-treatment years (1988 and 1990) were similar to patterns recorded previously. In 1988, the first scrape appeared Sept. 26, and in 1990, the first scrape was made Oct. 2. As expected, peak scraping during the control (non-treatment) years occurred the last week of October and the first week of November, when more than 50 percent of the season's total scraping occurred.

In 1989 (the first treatment year), the first scrape was made Sept. 6, less than 24 hours after I started mock scraping and adding buck urine. It escalated rapidly thereafter. I recorded 32 scrapes by Sept. 26, compared to only one during the same period the previous (non-treatment) year. Although buck response was not so dramatic the second treatment year (1991), bucks commenced scraping earlier (Sept. 9) than normal. Also, regardless of treatment, annual scraping activity peaked during the last week of October and first week of November.

Interestingly, bucks readily pawed my mock scrapes but were twice as likely to re-paw scrapes they initiated. In 1989, for example, bucks pawed 39 of 50 mock scrapes, but only six were repawed three or more times. By comparison, bucks converted 40 of 50 paired (untreated) limb sites into scrapes, 14 of which were they reopened three or more times.

For whatever reason, four mature enclosure bucks died from fighting injuries during this four-year study, and another died the next year. To my knowledge, no enclosure bucks died from fighting injuries during the previous 24 years. This leads me to believe my mock scrapes with urine from a foreign buck were at least partly to blame for the resultant social disruption.

Although application of buck urine to mock scrapes in early September induced earlier-than-normal scraping activity among enclosure bucks, the breeding dates of does weren't affected. Regardless of treatment, the first enclosure doe bred each year during the first week of November, and some didn't breed until December. In other words, earlier rutting behavior by bucks did not trigger early estrus in does.

CONCLUSIONS

The more we learn about whitetail signposting behavior, the more we realize how poorly understood it is. Although ground-pawing associated with scraping tends to be a seasonal phenomenon, some aspects of scraping behavior — such as limb scent-marking — apparently occur year-round. So the exact chemistry involved and the messages conveyed seem to change with the season.

Full-fledged scraping ability — complete with urination, ground-pawing and limb scent-marking — improves with buck age. So an abundance of scrapes immediately before peak whitetail breeding activity is a good indicator that mature bucks are around. But even mature bucks might vary in their scraping intensity, and the frequency with which they revisit their scrapes is seldom predictable.

Despite all the uncertainty, my studies demonstrate that mock scrapes really attract deer. You can make them as simple or complex as you wish. Often, it might require little more than placing a good overhead limb in the right place and letting bucks do the rest.

Logically, scraping away the duff and doctoring mock scrapes with lures such as deer urine or certain glandular secretions might increase buck visitation rates, but I can't prove it. ■

chapter 5

CUTTING-EDGE MOCK SCRAPES

STEVE BARTYLLA

▶ IN THE PAST FOUR YEARS, I've been blessed to take 15 mature bucks. Two came from public ground, and the rest came from primo private land. More than a quarter of them have been duped by mock scrapes.

Although I can't guarantee I wouldn't have arrowed any of them without mock scrapes, the ruses no doubt upped my odds. For example, the 163-inch Wisconsin buck I killed wasn't going to give me much time. I was caught without having my bow all the way up the tree yet, and things didn't look good.

However, the buck paused long enough at a mock scrape to allow me to nock an arrow. Settling the pin, I sent the arrow in flight that would fill my 2010 Wisconsin buck tag.

MORE SUCCESS

Want more reasons to try mock scrapes? Take the mature Minnesota 8-pointer I killed last year after chasing the buck around in circles.

Each time I'd see the buck, he'd enter the food plot from a different direction. It was big plot because of the size of the local deer population. Simply, it had to be a couple acres in size to withstand their feeding. Unfortunately, the plot's size also allowed this buck to feed away the few remaining minutes of light outside of shooting range.

I decided to cut down a small oak tree and plant it 20 yards in front of my stand. The goal was to create an obvious scrape tree that couldn't be resisted. Sure enough, it was the first place the mature buck headed for that evening. An arrow cut his scraping plans short.

Two seasons before, I killed another Minnesota buck using a deviation of the same method. That time, it was a limb nailed to a tree along the edge of an in-woods food plot. Calling brought the buck in, but the mock scrape turned the deer from head on to slightly quartering away, providing the lethal target I needed.

Then there was a tough Alberta bow hunt. For me, "tough" and "Alberta bow hunt" rarely belong in the same sentence. However, a late fall had left the in-woods food sources thriving and mature bucks were not venturing into the fields.

Despite putting out 20 scouting cameras and spending most mornings observing fields, I couldn't find a buck to hunt. I was getting frustrated. Finally, on Day 10 of the hunt, I spotted a large track adorning a mock scrape I'd made on the cut line about a half mile back in the timber. It was just a track, but at least I believed I'd finally found a mature buck. Four days later, I arrowed a heavy-antlered Northern Alberta 10-pointer less than 5 yards from that mock scrape.

REALISTIC EXPECTATIONS

Before we dig deeper, it would be irresponsible of me to not cover realistic expectations for mock scrapes. Too often hunters are sold empty promises on what tactics and products will deliver.

About 17 years ago, when I was first really getting into the outdoor industry, an insider took me under his wing. I can still recall watching him give a seminar before I was to take the stage. He was explaining to the audience that you simply can't make mock scrapes work unless you consistently use urine from a single buck. It just so happened he sold urines that were numbered with an identifier that linked it for life to the buck it came from. Using the same urine from the same buck all season long, it was nearly a lock you could tag the biggest buck in your area.

Two years later, I found myself waiting for the same speaker to wrap up before I could take the stage. He'd invented a can't-miss timed scrape dripper. Simply program it to release the packaged scent a half hour after you typically get in the tree and you were golden.

Apparently, I wasn't the only one that had seen his seminar two years before. At the end, when he was asked if the urine included with the dripper was numbered, his response floored me. "The scent included is enough to last two weeks," he explained. "If you haven't killed the biggest buck in your area by then, you're doing something wrong."

Later that night, I asked him how he could say such a thing. His response is something I'll never forget. "Steve," he said, "Most of these people will never shoot a trophy buck in their lifetime. Our job is to sell them on the dream of killing a trophy."

I don't sell dreams. If there is a way to make mock scrapes that will bring in every mature buck in the area, I don't know what it is.

However, I believe mock scrapes can be effective tools to tilt the odds for the hunter. That's exactly what they are though: tools. They won't change the world, but they can be difference makers.

In my opinion, most bucks that hit mock scrapes were already in the area, just not quite where the hunter needed them. The goal of a mock scrape is to pull bucks a short distance closer and position them for a potential shot.

TIMING YOUR RUSE

Although mock scrapes can be effective as early as July, I've found the first week or two in October to be the best time to start them. That gives the bucks a week or two to find them before scraping activities really starts to peak. That said, earlier never hurts.

SCOUTING TOOLS

Mock scrapes can also serve as effective scouting tools. In fact, I believe mock scrapes can be one of the more effective and overlooked scouting tools available. They are particularly valuable when the fall's leaf drop covers new sign in areas not previously hunted or scouted.

I first found myself in this situation while hunting a new area of public land about 15 years ago. A blanket of falling leaves had recently covered any ground sign. Rubs, some obvious food sources and understanding how deer use terrain were all I could base stand placement on. Unfortunately, because the area was hunted hard, I knew that setting up on the rubs around the food offered little chance of catching daylight movement.

Relying on topo maps and an educated guess on how the bucks would respond to pressure, I targeted seven topographical funnels that I believed showed promise for daylight movement. At each, I created mock scrapes.

The premise was simple. I'd return to each over the next few days with a stand on my back. If the scrape contained overly large tracks, I'd put the stand up and hunt.

It worked. By the end, the tracks had told me to setup on three of the seven funnels. Not only were buck sightings high, only an unseen branch spared the life of one mid-140s buck. An 8-pointer that measured more than 140 wasn't so lucky.

The reason mock scrapes work so well for this is that, during the scraping phase of season, it seems that a well-placed licking branch and large oval of fresh dirt are too much for bucks to resist checking. It's almost like a reflex that when that mock scrape stands out, they need to check it.

CREATING MOCK SCRAPES

If a hunter gets creative, there are many ways to create a suitable licking branch nearly anywhere one is needed. Existing branches can be bent down and cut branches can be stapled to trees or even hung from a wire strung between two existing trees.

I'll cover how to create a mock scrape by cutting and "planting" a tree. However, it can be modified to any version of getting a licking branch at the nose level of a passing buck.

1) Select and cut a suitable tree. Its diameter is best in the 4- to 6-inch range and should offer a licking branch 7- to 8-feet above the cut. When possible, use species that are commonly used for scraping in the area, but most any species will work.

2) Cut off the top a couple inches above the licking branch to reduce weight. Also trim the branches below. If you will be using a scrape dripper, leaving a branch above the licking branch to tie it to is a nice touch, but the dripper can also be tied to the licking branch itself. Doing so doesn't hurt the mock scrape's effectiveness, but bucks can beat the scrape dripper up a little.

3) Dig a 2- to 3-foot hole slightly bigger than the tree's diameter. Post hole diggers work well.

4) Point the licking branch toward where your stand will be located.

5) With a branch, rake or hoe, create a 3- to 5-foot oval of dirt below the licking branch, placing its center just out from directly beneath the tip of the branch.

6) If using a scent dripper, attach it so that the scent will drip down onto the dirt.

A nice technique to get into a buck's head is to use immature buck urine until about four days before your hunt. At that point, switch to dominant buck urine and pour some estrus scent into the scrape. Freshen the scrape with estrus scent

when hunting it. This sends the message that a new buck has emerged and is set to steal a ready doe. About 15 percent of the time I use this technique, the area gets tore up with new rubs and scrapes.

UPPING THE ODDS

It's the reflex-like reaction that also makes mock scrapes valuable hunting tools. It doesn't take much thought to envision how drawing bucks short distances and positioning them can be extremely helpful.

Whether you are hunting a farm field, oversized food plot, meadow, clear cut regrowth or nearly any other open area you can't completely cover with a bow, a scrape tree "planted" in the open draws attention. It's almost like the drawing power the gaudiest casino on the Las Vegas strip possesses, with its pulsating lights drawing gamblers like a magnet.

A scrape tree 20 yards out in front of a stand can be very effective. No, this trick won't always draw every buck to the spot, but it is sure to draw in considerably more bucks than would normally visit that specific location.

Whether it's "planting" a scrape tree in the open or using an existing limb back in the woods, mock scrapes also should be used to position bucks for the shot.

Two things I almost always do are place the scrape 20 yards away and point the licking branch to my stand. That way, I have both a yardage marker and I am positioning the buck for a broadside or quartering away shot. Almost no buck investigating it will be presenting the dreaded quartering-to orientation. That alone ups my odds of a kill.

As an added bonus, this orientation directs the buck's attention away from the stand. Obviously, this allows for more undetected movements.

Finally, the act of checking the scrape not only stops the buck for the shot, eliminating the need for me to put him on alert with a grunt, but it also provides extra time for the shot itself, while the buck works the scrape.

CONCLUSION

None of these benefits are world changers. However, add them all together and mock scrapes simply increase the odds of turning close encounters into kills. As serious hunters, that's really about as world changing as it realistically gets. ∎

chapter 6

READING THE RUB

CHARLES J. ALSHEIMER

▶ OCT. 6, 2012: DAWN ARRIVED cool and overcast, just the right conditions for photographing autumn whitetails. My plan that morning was to set up near a prime clover field in hopes of photographing any deer behavior that might occur. I didn't have to wait long. A half hour after shooting light, a mature 10-pointer inched his way across the field, eventually working to a patch of goldenrod and staghorn sumac saplings, close to where I was set up.

Every few feet, the buck paused to smell some of the goldenrod stems and blossoms. When he came to the first sumac, he paused and then began rubbing his moist nose up and down the 2-inch sapling, leaving a smear of saliva on the bark. Within seconds, he began to gently nibble on the sumac's tender bark with his incisor teeth. When two small strips were removed, the big buck started rubbing his antlers on the sapling, slowly at first, but 30 seconds into the rubbing ritual, his pace grew intense. As the buck leaned into the sapling, he feverishly thrust his antlers up and down the sumac's trunk, causing the swaying tree's leaves to rain down around him. Through the camera's lens, I saw shreds of bark flaking off and falling to the ground What didn't land in the grass clung to the buck's antlers. Every 10 seconds or so, the buck would stop rubbing long enough to smell and rub his nose against the scarred sapling to deposit scent. After five minutes of rubbing, smelling and licking the rub, the 10-pointer walked off into the woods, his antlers covered with shredded bark.

Quickly, I hit the camera LCD screen's review button to see the photos I'd taken. Before I could finish, I picked up movement of something coming through the goldenrod cover. It was another deer — a mature buck. Cautiously, the buck made his way to the tattered rub and peered in the direction the big 10-pointer had gone. Sensing there was no threat of the dominant buck's return, the other buck smelled the skinned-up rub and then began rubbing. For almost five minutes, the buck followed the same ritual as the 10-pointer by going from rubbing to licking to smelling. When he finally finished shredding sumac, he wandered off in the opposite direction of the 10-pointer. Needless to say, by the time the two bucks had done their rubbing, the sapling was destroyed.

Though I have seen multiple bucks work the same rub in the past, I've never seen two mature bucks trash a tree so fast during my years of photography. When I examined the site, I was struck by the amount of bark shavings on the ground and the way the sumac's branches had been broken. What I had witnessed in little more than 15 minutes is only one example of a whitetail's rubbing behavior.

Here's what I've learned about the whitetail's rubbing behavior from more than 50 years of hunting and photographing whitetails.

RUBS SEND A MESSAGE

Humans learn by seeing. Deer do, too. When a hunter comes upon a big rub, his heart skips a beat. When a whitetail buck encounters a rub of any size, it has different thoughts. Our excitement has to do with hunting possibilities. A buck's has to do with identifying who made the rub, because their world is all about competition.

When a buck makes a rub, he deposits liberal amounts of scent from his nasal, preorbital and forehead gland on the sapling or tree. The number of rubs a buck makes in his home range depends on several factors, such as how sexually active he is, the number of adult does in his core area and the number of bucks in his home range (especially 2½-plus-year-old bucks). Simply, scent drives a buck, and the more scent they leave in their travels, the greater the possibility for an intense rut.

I've learned from more than 20 years of raising whitetails that every deer has its own distinct odor, which is identifiable to other deer living in their core area. So when a buck makes a rub, other bucks and does can identify which buck made the rub by the scent left on the rub. Because of this, it's not uncommon for several bucks to work the same rub within hours of each other to share their identity and dominance.

SIZE MATTERS

Few things get a hunter more excited than seeing a huge rub on a tree more than 4 inches in diameter. In more than 90 percent of the cases, such rubs are made by a mature buck. I say this because in more than 40 years of photographing whitetails, I can count on one hand how many times I've seen a yearling buck rubbing a tree more than 4 inches in diameter. Given a choice, yearling bucks opt to make rubs on saplings and trees smaller than 2 inches in diameter, with a heavy preference to trees less than 1 inch in diameter.

Mature bucks rub to leave scent on anything from pencil-sized saplings to 1-foot-diameter trees. Some of the rubs mature bucks make on bigger trees will develop into what are called traditional sign-post rubs. These are rubs normally 4-plus inches in diameter (at waist level) along habitat edges and trails and are worked by bucks year after year, usually until the tree dies from being rubbed so much. In nearly every place I've ever hunted or photographed, I've found such rubs, and most are very impressive.

During my career I've photographed bucks making rubs on goldenrod stems, corn stalks, fence posts, telephone poles, a variety of tree species and even a photographer's tripod.

PREFERENCE AND LOCATION

During the past 40 years, much research has gone into the species of trees bucks prefer to rub. My experience has revealed that species preference is region specific. Here in western New York, bucks tend to prefer smooth-bark trees, which also happen to be their preferred browse species. As a result, apple, aspen, cherry, hemlock, black locust, red cedar, red oak, staghorn sumac and soft maple make up most of the rubs in my area. In addition, saplings and trees with no branches for the first four feet are preferred most often.

In 1995, my family built a 35-acre enclosure on our farm to study deer behavior. Since then, I've conducted several studies to see if the enclosure bucks have a rubbing preference for certain tree species. By cutting 7- to 8-foot saplings (2 inches or so in diameter, of various tree species) and placing them 1½ feet in the ground, I've determined that the aroma given off by a tree species plays a significant role in rubbing preference. When given a choice, the bucks in our enclosure almost always rub, in this order, staghorn sumac, apple, black locust, hemlock, red cedar and aspen before rubbing on maple, red and white oak, or American beech. However, it should be pointed out that if a buck is in the mood to rub, it will rub on any tree species, regardless of whether it is alive or dead. For example, there are several wooden fence posts in the enclosure that are rubbed each fall. And one of the biggest rubs I have ever seen in the wild was on a 6-inch diameter fence post in Saskatchewan.

Most rubs will be found in travel corridors, along field edges, next to fence openings or logging roads, or along breaks in habitat, such as where a swamp butts up to open hardwoods. An exception might occur during a fall in which there is a heavy acorn crop. In heavy mast areas, rubbing will occur wherever acorns are falling.

5 TYPES OF RUBS

1. Licking stick: Random in nature, a licking stick is a rub made on a sapling about the size of your pinky finger. During the rubbing process, a buck often breaks the sapling off two to three feet off the ground while rubbing and tangling it in his antlers. Because of the small size of licking sticks, hunters seldom notice them, but deer do. In some cases, a buck will rub a licking stick for several minutes, leaving a tremendous amount of scent behind.

2. Random rub: Rubs made by bucks as they cruise their home range. They have no pattern to them and can vary greatly in size. In most cases, they will not be revisited.

3. Rub-line rubs: Multiple rubs made by mature bucks through their commonly used corridors, usually between their bedding and feeding areas. Such rubs can be seen within sight of each other and can be great places to ambush a buck.

4. Breeding party rubs: A cluster of rubs made in a relatively small area during the breeding phase of the rut, where several bucks have formed for breeding rights to an estrous doe.

5. Traditional sign-post rub: Rubs typically 4-plus inches in diameter (at waist height) along travel corridors used by bucks and does. These rubs are used by multiple bucks year after year. They usually stay active until the tree finally dies or grows too large to be rubbed anymore.

COMPETITIVE SIGN-POSTING

When their velvet is peeled, bucks begin making rubs randomly throughout their home range. As the rut nears, rubbing frequency intensifies along trails, ridge lines or areas through which bucks commonly travel. If an area's antlered-buck-to-

adult-doe-ratio is balanced, competition will be great for breeding rights. In such locations, rubbing sign will seem to explode during the two- to three-week period before peak breeding. During this time, bucks have a tendency to check out fresh rubs to determine who made it, and it's not uncommon for them to rework the rub. Also, it's not uncommon for does to check out rubs and smell, lick and rub their foreheads and necks on rubs during the weeks leading up to breeding.

When the breeding phase of the rut explodes, breeding parties form when several bucks are vying to breed the same doe. Such a setting might find an estrous doe bedded, with a dominant buck standing or bedded nearby, while subordinate bucks circle the pair from a distance. Throughout the doe's 24-hour estrus period (when she will be bred) the breeding party might not move 100 yards. During this time, many scrapes and rubs will be made by dominant and subordinate bucks as a way to show each other their dominance. Every time I've photographed such an event or checked the sign left behind, I'm amazed by how torn up the area appears and how many rubs have been made in a relatively small area.

GATEWAY TO SUCCESS?

When looking at a rub, check it for any interesting characteristics that will reveal something different about the buck that made it. How high are the gouges on the bark? If they are higher than normal and some higher branches are broken off, a mature buck was obviously working it over.

Not all rubs are candidates for hunting. Rubs along field edges were probably made randomly at night, especially if your hunting area receives a lot of hunting pressure. Rubs made a distance from feeding areas will be hunting candidates. In addition, you might be able to determine a buck's travel route by the rub's position. In most cases, a buck will rub on the side of the tree from which he approached. This reveals the direction he was most likely traveling. Rubs can also tip you off about the time of day they were made. A rub that faces a bedding area was probably made in the evening, when the buck was heading toward a feeding area. If the rub faces away from a bedding area, it was most likely made in the morning as a buck was traveling back to bed.

Last, don't rule out hunting close to a traditional sign-post rub. In areas where mature bucks are prevalent, finding sign-post rubs can increase your chances of hunting a slammer buck come fall. ■

chapter 7

ARE YOU OVERHUNTING YOUR FOOD PLOTS?

MATT HARPER

▶ I AM SURE YOU HAVE heard the phrase, "Going one too many times to the well." The saying relates to doing the exact same thing over and over with decreasing instances of success.

Most of us are guilty of going to the well too often in one thing or another, and for good reason. The success experienced early on was so great that it makes it tempting to continue doing the same thing even when the results change. We think to ourselves, "Maybe one more time ... surely it will work again this time." Most times, however, it does not work. In fact, the results usually become progressively worse.

Hunters are not immune to this phenomenon either. Say, for instance, that you have killed a big buck out of one particular stand two years in a row. You know darned well you will be in that stand when the season rolls around again. When the big buck doesn't show himself the first two or three times, the memory of those big bucks from years past is so powerful that you stick with it in the hopes another one will eventually appear. In fact, each time you sit in the stand you see progressively fewer deer.

The same can happen when hunting near food plots. Maybe you go through a stretch of days when you see a big buck enter your food plot at one particular spot. There are no trees big enough to place a stand in that spot, so you pop up a ground blind in hopes of ambushing the buck. You then lock yourself to that blind "knowing" he will come out once again.

He doesn't; at least not while you're sitting there.

This last scenario is the most common example of going to the well one too many times while hunting. After considering all the work we do to turn barren land into lush food plots, it's easy to see how we "fall in love" with these spots ... and quickly burn them out.

That picturesque, emerald-green food plot starkly set against the timber line awash in fall color just looks like a place a big buck should be at dawn and dusk. However, that's not how it usually goes down. To experience consistent success, you must always adapt and change your strategies.

HUNTING NEAR FOOD PLOTS

I am not suggesting you should never hunt near a food plot. Regardless if a plot is designed as a hunting plot or nutritional plot, there are certainly instances that would behoove one to hunt directly over the food source. Timing and strategy, however, are both critical components to increasing the odds of killing a mature buck.

In terms of timing, early season and late season will typically produce the best chance of a mature buck showing up during daylight. During the early season, bucks are still in their summer feeding patterns, and their movements are controlled by their stomachs more than their libido.

The late season is probably the best time to hunt directly over a food plot. Bucks are coming off their rut diet (little to no food intake and a great expense of energy) and are frantically trying to put on weight before winter.

The more frigid the conditions, the more likely an old buck will break from his reclusive habits and venture onto a field during daylight. There can also be instances during the rut when an evening sit can be productive. If does are feeding in a plot and bucks are checking and chasing, you might have a quick opportunity.

I have also experienced good results hunting over plots when the rut has an unexpected slowdown. If the weather turns warm during the rut, bucks will sometimes take the opportunity to replenish their energy reserves. In 2010, the weather didn't change where I was hunting, but I noticed a decrease in buck sightings at my normal rut stands. I checked on some food plots and saw several good bucks feeding during daylight. This went on for about three days until they switched to a more typical rut pattern. My guess is those three or four days were in between major estrous cycles, and the bucks were taking the opportunity to feed. This is a fairly common occurrence during the rut, but it's difficult to pinpoint exactly when and how long it will occur. There are no definitive times between estrous cycles when all bucks will feed.

STAY HIDDEN

If you are going to hunt directly over a food plot, the most critical aspect to your strategy is remaining undetected. Most of us have experienced the disappointment of ever-decreasing deer numbers on consecutive visits to the same food-plot stand. The first time we sit there, we see tons of deer and from all segments of the herd — bucks and does; fawns, yearlings and older deer. The next time we hunt, we see a few young bucks and some does and fawns. By the third or fourth sit, all that shows up are yearling bucks and maybe a young doe and her fawns. What happened? You have effectively burned out your food plot from a hunting perspective.

If you have scouted a particular buck, early season might offer better odds than during the rut. Early season bucks will be focussing on food and, hence, be more predictable. However, the slightest bad vibe they detect while approaching the plot will cause them to visit the plot only after dark; or they might even move to a different food source.

I have found that no matter how careful you are, two (maybe three) early season sits on the same food plot is about all you can expect before a mature buck figures out that hunting season has started. Late season offers a bit more leniency because the threat of starvation can overcome a buck's wariness. However, even during late

season, busting deer while sitting over the field will result in diminishing numbers of deer feeding during daylight.

To minimize the odds of burning out a food plot, you must do all you can to stay clear of a buck's senses. First, do whatever you can to place your stand in a position where you can get to and from the stand without detection. Most food-plot hunts will occur in the evening, so getting to the stand undetected might be fairly easy. Getting out of the stand with a dozen or more sets of eyes on you is another matter. Use ditches, creek beds, tree rows, etc. to get to your stand unseen — even if it takes you on a winding route instead of a direct path. In the absence of such cover, I have planted rows of corn or tall cane to help hide my journey to a plot stand.

You can also design your plots with a stand location in mind that allows you to get into the stand unseen (such as "S" shaped plots that create dead spots). Scent control is a must when hunting plot stands. Never hunt a plot stand when the wind is wrong. A young buck or doe might come back to a field the next evening even though they caught a whiff of you, but odds are an old buck will not. I normally have at least two different stand setups for plots so that I have options depending on the wind direction.

HUNTING OFF THE PLOT

If you visit my farm you will see several stand setups designed to hunt directly over food plots. But during most of pre-rut and rut, you will likely not see me sitting in one of them. Venture off the field 50 to 100 yards — or find a bottle-necked funnel connecting two different food sources — and you will find the stands I use during the pre-rut and the rut.

As the rut nears, a buck's drive to breed trumps his growling belly and he is constantly on the move looking for a doe that is agreeable to companionship. Does this mean that bucks will never visit food plots? Actually, bucks visit food plots more frequently during this time of year than any other. Remember, bucks are looking for does, and does are always looking for food. This is the time of year bucks travel from plot to plot scent-checking fields and trails leading to the plots.

If you scout the perimeter of most plots, you will find major travel trails that connect bedding and travel corridors. Look closely and you likely find a much fainter trail that circles the boundary of the plot that bisects the major trails. This faint trail is the one used by bucks as they cruise the edges of feeding areas checking each major trail for receptive does. If you are sitting directly on the plot during this phase of the breeding cycle, you will likely not see these cruising bucks. Exactly how far off the food plot you will find this trail varies from plot to plot, so each plot needs to be scouted to determine stand location.

If prevailing winds are out of the west, the most-used buck trails will be along the eastern side of the plot. Travel corridors and funnels that connect two food plots are also great places for stand setups to catch cruising bucks. Additionally, bucks will cruise the edges of doe bedding areas much like they do with food plots. Placing stands or blinds that allow you to hunt these edges can also be productive.

What does this have to do with blowing out food plots? First, if the goal is harvest a mature buck then you need to be in the most likely place to give you an opportunity. Just because the food plot is 100 yards away, doesn't mean that the plot isn't helping you get the drop on that buck. The food plot will greatly increase the odds that bucks will be around somewhere in that vicinity.

Second, if you hunt the food plot all season, you will be more likely to burn out that area. Finally, a buck is likely to move around the perimeter of a plot while scent-checking the field. If you are sitting on the field, the buck will most likely figure out that you are in your favorite spot again.

CONCLUSION

Food plots can definitely improve the quality of your deer herd and increase the odds of a successful hunting season. However, implementing the correct food plot hunting strategies will influence the manifestation of food plot benefits.

Hunt food plots incorrectly, and you will likely be sitting over of a beautiful but empty field. Hunt them correctly, and the food plot will likely exhibit the full hunting potential that it can produce. ■

chapter 8

7 STRATEGIES FOR BEATING THE OCTOBER LULL

TOM CARPENTER

▶ DO YOU BELIEVE IN THE October lull?

Here's one way to define the term. October lull describes what happens to white-tailed deer movement during autumn's peak month. Late-summer movement patterns have ended, largely related to a shift in deer foods and their availability. But the rut's action, followed by the more settled and patternable conditions of late season, are far off. Whitetails are in a time of transition, and it's difficult for hunters to figure them out and get a good setup going.

Here's another way to define the term. October lull describes what happens to white-tailed deer hunters during autumn's peak month. Blaming decreased deer sightings on a perceived drop in deer movement, hunters approach the challenge in one of two ways — both of them lulls in their own right. October whitetail chasers either keep hunting like they did in the early season, praying for a change in luck or a pick-up in deer activity. Or they sit on the sidelines in anticipation of the upcoming rut, thereby wasting some prime weeks of hunting.

Which definition do you buy into? There's truth in both concepts ... but also some misconceptions.

The key words in those October lull definitions are *time of transition* and *perceived drop in deer movement*. Deer movement isn't depressed in October; it's merely changing. The only real lull is what's not happening at the same old spot you've been watching since the leaves were green. And there's no reason for a self-imposed hunting lull "until the rut kicks in." Considering the vagaries of weather and myriad other uncontrollables, there are no guarantees whatsoever in that plan B.

So what are we left with? October ...and seven strategies for getting after your venison when full autumn has settled over the land, the leaves are ablaze, and the whitetails are proving to be their usual wary, persnickety, hard-to-figure-out selves.

PLAY THE ACORN GAME

The deer have been hitting the green fields hard and then one day — POOF! — the whitetails vanish. What happened? One likely answer is, the acorns are dropping and the deer have shifted their feeding focus. If there's one menu item whitetails like more than their salad, it's acorns with all their abundant protein (for energy and building muscle mass) and calories (for building fat) as deer gird for the upcoming winter.

So, do you set up right in the oaks, or on a travel corridor to or from them? It all depends on time of day.

October hunting is aggressive hunting. One option is to set up right at the source: in the oaks themselves. That's why afternoon hunts in the oaks are great — get there plenty early, set up, settle in, and be quietly waiting when the deer start moving.

A dawn hunt in the oaks is tough, because the deer may already be there feeding when you arrive. So hunt travel corridors coming out of the oaks. But don't be afraid to move right into the oaks after a couple hours. A mid-morning stand among the acorns are can be a fine place to arrow a hungry October whitetail.

HIT THE CROP HARVEST

Here's another food play for October.

In corn country, the crop harvest really shifts whitetail habits and movement patterns. This is good news in two ways:

1. Chopping down all that corn eliminates endless acres of extra whitetail hiding places. The deer become more visible, and you have a shot at figuring them out.

2. Whitetails find a new and accessible food source in the stubble. Become a combine watcher, and hit it right after the harvest.

Corn is second only to acorns in October's preferred food hierarchy. The protein content isn't as high as in acorns, but all the sugar and carbohydrates in corn really pack on the winter fat, and whitetails know it.

Spend an evening glassing where the whitetails approach a fresh-cut cornfield, then set up on their approach. You can also hunt the field itself, especially any secluded nooks, swales, crannies or corners where the deer like to sneak out and start feeding a little early.

THE SOFT MAST CONNECTION

Hard mast — mainly acorns, but also hickory nuts, beechnuts, chestnuts and others — gets all the attention. But don't overlook soft mast as a prime food source to focus on when hunting October whitetails. While the window of availability may be brief, the opportunity can be intense. Soft mast is like candy to whitetails. Look for:

Apples. Never pass up a couple fruit-laden apple trees, or a whole orchard of them. Apples sweeten and drop with October frosts.

Persimmons. Southern hunters know how ripening persimmons pull deer in. This happens around mid-October.

Crabapples. Don't overlook patches of these productive trees.

Pears. Sweet, soft pears may be the biggest soft-mast deer magnet of all!

One final note: If you own or help manage some hunting land, consider planting soft mast trees like those mentioned above. They can really pull in October whitetails.

HUNT LIKE IT'S THE RUT

The farther into October, the closer you get to full rutting action. The last week of October is really rutting time across much of whitetail country. So what's going on breeding-wise during the first three weeks of the month?

The answer is: The bucks are warming up and marking territory. By mid-month you're starting to see scrapes. In reality, the rut is all ready to go, and the bucks are ready to breed.

So hunt like it's the rut. Figure out those rub or scrape lines. Set up in high traffic areas or travel funnels. Grunt some. Rattle a little — though don't try to imitate an all-out buck brawl yet. A little tine tickling is the ticket — just enough to get a buck curious. He isn't quite ready to fight yet, but he's willing to check out who is.

Finally, any time in October is prime time for using doe-in-heat scents. Some does are in fact starting to come into estrus now. It's nature's way of spreading out springtime's whitetail "hatch" with a few early births next spring, in case the main fawn drop for some reason is a disaster. (This is also the biological reason there's a late or December rut as well.)

EMPLOY A DECOY

October is the perfect time to get some use out of that deer decoy. Your local whitetails probably haven't seen one yet this year, and the first time can really get the deers' attention up and their curiosity chugging. Bucks are ready for breeding now. The curiosity factor and the breeding urge call for an antlerless decoy.

If you're in the market to shoot an antlerless deer for the freezer, which I always am, a doe decoy can also do that job. Most groups of antlerless whitetails that are hanging around together in October are family groups. Adult does will come check out the newcomer to their territory, offering you a shot.

Place decoys on field edges and at other highly visible spots where traveling or feeding deer can see them. That visibility is key. Set up so the wind is blowing from the decoy to you, but also make sure you can swing and shoot cross-wind, as bucks and does alike will often sidle in, trying to get the breeze in their favor, and you'll need to make your shot before they circle downwind.

DEER TALK

You can also drum up some October action by making deer sounds. This approach works for two reasons. One, bucks are as attracted to audio breeding cues as they are olfactory ones. Two, doe talk can get antlerless deer coming in, if you a have a doe tag you want to fill.

As the month wears on, you might do more (and more aggressive) grunting and buck challenges. But earlier on, the goal is to make doe talk:

•Doe estrus bleats. Sound a doe makes when she's ready to breed. October bucks are interested in some easy action.

•Fawn bleats. Good any time, but especially in October, for calling in mature does.

•Fawn distress bawls. May bring in curious does for a look.

HUNT OTHER OPENERS

Some bowhunters lament the start of pheasant, squirrel or fall turkey seasons because all the hunting activity inundates the countryside with humans chasing other critters, which disrupts whitetail movements. But why not think of these small armies as your own personal pushers, and use them to your advantage?

Think about where these bird, small game and turkey hunters ply their trade. Get out early and set up in escape cover where whitetails will head. Hunt the day out. That's important: While the initial push of duck, pheasant or squirrel hunter activity might not result in a deer in your sights right away, the whitetails will often spend the rest of the day filtering back in after making their flanking moves.

On Wisconsin's pheasant opener, my brothers and I used to skirt a lake and set up on a couple dry islands in a secluded swamp were the bird-hunting armies wouldn't tread. Not long after noon on opening day, after the shotguns started popping in the grasslands, the whitetails would start filtering into the bottoms as they evaded the circus. I really like pheasant hunting, but this was always a good trade, and it livened up a mid-October bowhunting day.

HUNT LIKE IT'S HOT

There is one legitimate reason that whitetail movement might truly be inhibited in early to mid October: Deer are already sporting their winter coats, and even a day that seems cool to you or me might way too warm for a whitetail to do much traveling. Bring out a warm October sun with balmy Indian summer air and you could have the local deer herd going pretty nocturnal on you.

Anything below 50 F won't depress much whitetail activity. Between 50 and 60 F, you might still get some daytime movement. Above 60 F is pretty warm for a whitetail in its thick winter coat.

Of course, there's not much you can do to hunt deer that are moving only at night. But one solution is to hunt lowlands near water — riverbottoms, creeks, springs and ponds. It's cooler and shadier here, and deer need the water too. Another approach is to make your afternoon setup in timber, instead of on field edges, to have a chance at getting deer in your sights while they're staging.

Finally, keep your schedule flexible. Plan to hunt on days when a front blows through and the weather cools off. This can cause a big spike in whitetail activity. The deer will often stay out later in the morning, and come out earlier in the evening, when the air is cooler and more autumn-like.

CONCLUSION

It's too easy to call October a wash and sit at home, waiting for the rut and the "good hunting" to begin. The whitetails are out there now. You just have to change up your approach, get a little more aggressive, get out there with a plan to beat October's supposed lull, and hunt. ∎

chapter 9

DEER RESEARCH:
LULL TO CHAOS

JOHN J. OZOGA

▶ WHITE-TAILED DEER ARE SHORT-DAY BREEDERS; they breed in autumn when day length (photoperiod) is decreasing. It is this autumn decrease in the amount of daylight that triggers sharp seasonal changes in deer physiology, behavior, and nutritional requirements.

The whitetail's breeding window is narrow in the North, but widens southward until breeding takes place year-round near the equator. As a result, variations in commencement and duration of the rut can be expected from North to South.

Hunters commonly refer to the period immediately preceding breeding as the "pre-rut" — a unique period when deer behavior can change overnight, requiring equally unique and versatile hunting tactics.

Obviously, pre-rut terminates when breeding starts. But when does it start? How does deer behavior change during the course of the pre-rut? And, more importantly, precisely what exact changes take place in deer behavior that hunters should be alert to and can take advantage of?

DIFFERING VIEWS

A search of the scientific literature reveals a scarcity of reference to the pre-rut period and virtually no summary of events involved. At least one reference, from Texas, suggests the pre-rut commences four to six weeks before the first does breed.

Even deer experts tend to vary in their views concerning the pre-rut. For example, in a *Deer & Deer Hunting* article Charles Alsheimer discussed in detail the so-called "September lull, October lull or pre-rut lull" when bucks seem to be especially inactive, secretive and difficult to hunt.

Conversely, when I quizzed noted deer researcher Karl Miller regarding his interpretation of the pre-rut, he dwelled upon the two-week period immediately before the first does breed. This is when something — presumably inherent physiological changes — takes place that literally causes an explosion in deer activity like at no other time during the year.

Based upon Northern research experience, I admittedly have my own biased views concerning the whitetail pre-rut. Here in the Upper Peninsula of Michigan, winter weather dictates seasonal changes in deer behavior. It seems whitetails are either recovering from the winter season, enduring it or preparing for the next winter. There is no room for renegade deer behavior based on fluctuations in moon phase, temperature, precipitation or any other such factor that might fluctuate wildly and/ or unpredictably from one year to the next. If whitetails are to survive in this precarious environment, they must follow their genetically selected plan, and behave accordingly.

Be that as it may, here's the way I see it.

COMMENCEMENT OF PRE-RUT

One can argue as to when the pre-rut starts, because whitetails exhibit a host of physiological changes — and resultant behavioral changes — at this time of year. Depending upon the region, some of these changes can be subtle and difficult to identify; they can also be influenced by environmental (temperature, precipitation, etc.) or social factors (herd density, sex-age, etc.). Hence, pinpointing commencement of the pre-rut can be arguable.

Rising levels of the male sex hormone testosterone lead to antler maturation, velvet stripping and striking changes in buck behavior. In my view, the timing of this process among mature bucks signals commencement of the pre-rut. Although velvet shedding dates vary among bucks, depending upon their age and health status (i.e., young and poorly fed bucks tend to shed late), some mature individuals on Northern range always shed antler velvet about September 1, annually — some even a few days earlier.

Typically, reproductively experienced does that failed to raise fawns the previous spring are the first to conceive, generally during the last week of October.

In my opinion, given these antler velvet shedding and conception dates, the Northern pre-rut lasts seven to eight weeks — from the first of September until the end of October.

SOCIAL BEHAVIOR

White-tailed deer live in complex social arrangements, where such things as dominance rank and social alliances sometimes determine whether an individual deer lives or dies. Adult whitetails also exhibit sexual segregation: bucks and does live apart much of the year, but associations change with the seasons.

Separation of the adult sexes is most pronounced during the fawn-rearing period, when does with newborns exhibit territorial behavior and social isolation by driving away all other deer from the area, including other family members. Generally, this period of aggressive isolation lasts six to eight weeks, depending upon herd density.

The pre-rut period is characterized by reunion of related females and their young, intermixing of the adult sexes, and intense socialization. Sparring among bucks gradually gives way to more serious push fighting and establishment of buck dominance hierarchies. Aggression among does and their yearling male offspring encourages male dispersal to new range. Young unproductive females, on the other

hand, are more likely become subordinate to a matriarch doe and reunite with the family group.

Such mixed gatherings, which might involve a hundred or more deer, usually take place in select open areas during evening and at night in September. Although it's generally assumed such socializing occurs chiefly in response to concentrated nutritious forage, such behavior undoubtedly serves other vitally important social functions.

Openings, while maybe not absolutely essential from a behavioral standpoint, serve deer a very special purpose during the pre-rut. When interspersed throughout densely forested habitat, openings permit deer to gather, socialize and visually communicate. Open areas void of predators serve as arenas where bucks can display, spar with one another, engage in serious fights to decide dominance, if necessary, and communicate their social status to prospective mates and competitors alike.

This habit of early pre-rut congregating makes local deer population assessment via nighttime spotlighting especially rewarding.

But remember, some deer might come a long way to join such festivities and be elsewhere a month later. By mid-October most such grouping is over; families return to their traditional haunts and bucks become solitary travelers often covering areas several square miles in size.

For the dedicated student of deer behavior, these highly observable pre-rut changes in deer behavior are fascinating to watch. However, the late October-early November deer hunter might become frustrated, wondering where that monster buck went.

ACTIVITY LEVELS

Normally, whitetails exhibit two seasonal activity peaks: during times of birthing and breeding. Their lowest level of activity occurs during summer, when nutritious foods are readily available and during winter when deer are less active in order to conserve energy. During studies conducted in Lower Michigan's George Reserve, percent of daily deer activity ranged from 21 percent on Feb. 6 to 82 percent on Oct. 18.

Given the sharp changes in buck activity that take place during pre-rut, it's tempting to refer to a "lull" in deer activity during early pre-rut. In reality, the level of activity deer exhibit during September and early October is somewhat elevated as compared to that during summer. By comparison, it's the sharp rise in deer activity that takes place during late pre-rut and early rut (late October-early November) that is so outstanding.

ACTIVITY RHYTHMS

Whitetails tend to be corpuscular (most active around dawn and dusk). Some deer might show additional minor peaks of activity during midday and twice at night, and follow a distinct five-peaked daily rhythm. However, the times of peak activity for individual deer might differ, depending upon age, reproductive status, general health, metabolic needs and environmental factors. As a result, individual secondary activity peaks might not be synchronized.

In the George Reserve studies, deer of either sex had similar daily activity rhythms during most months. However, during September and October, bucks were more active than does at night, and does were more active than bucks during the day. The biological significance of this is unclear, but is probably related to differences in nutritional requirements and the approaching rut. For example, some behavior, like making scrapes, is done primarily at night.

NUTRITION

Like other seasonal events in the whitetail's life, the accumulation of fat is cued by photoperiod and controlled by hormones. As day length shortens, deer become more active, eat more and accumulate fat.

During the pre-rut, high energy foods such as lush forbs, soft and hard mast, and agricultural crops are favored. Understandably, such energy-rich foods tend to be concentrated, causing equally concentrated deer activity. Or, sometimes such nutritious foods might be scarce, slowing the rate of fattening and increasing feeding activity.

Autumn is a critical time for Northern whitetails. Food quality and quantity typically decrease, fawns must reach their maximum size and deer must accumulate fat reserves for winter.

Does not burdened with nursing fawns experience less overall energy drain, molt before and gain weight faster than does with fawns. Because fawns must physically mature and fatten simultaneously, they seldom achieve their peak weight until December.

Adult bucks usually begin fattening before other deer — in July. As a result, mature bucks often reach their peak weight by early October. They are also the first to grow their winter coat, usually in early September.

In Alabama, bucks were less frequently photographed than expected with trail-cameras during the early pre-rut. The researchers speculated that fattened adult bucks exhibit a suppression in activity during the pre-rut, possibly in anticipation of excessive energy demands associated with the breeding season.

In my studies, conducted in northern Michigan, bucks stayed longer, on average, per feeder visit in September (about 16 minutes) than at any other time during the year.

Deer living on poor quality summer-fall range might not have the luxury of a pre-rut lull in feeding activity. Likewise, those experiencing drought might have difficulty accumulating the critical amount of fat prior to the rut. Hence, regional differences in early pre-rut buck movement and feeding activity, as well as response to bait, can be expected.

SILENT OVULATION

Everything abruptly changes during mid-October. Almost overnight, bucks seem to go berserk. Scraping activity escalates, and bucks won't tolerate each other as they wildly chase every doe in sight. All semblance of social order vanishes — or so it seems — as belligerent bucks scurry in all directions day and night, testing every doe they find.

A number of species, including whitetails, demonstrate a condition referred to as "silent ovulation." This is when the female shows histological and physiological signs of estrus, including ovulation, but not the mating response, or psychological heat. It appears to be most common in first time breeders and usually occurs about two weeks before mating.

Some researchers, including myself, believe silent estrus might mysteriously spur the whitetail's crazy behavior a couple of weeks before breeding begins — starting about mid-October.

In other words, a doe's silent ovulation might emit pheromones that alert and excite bucks to her pending condition, but she won't be in the mood to mate and will flee the bucks' advances. It takes little imagination to envision the havoc — and favorable hunting conditions — that would result if several (pubertal) does entered this attractive, but elusive, state at the same time.

SIGNPOSTING

With a forest-dwelling animal like the whitetail, glandular secretions and scent-marking, referred to as chemical signals, play an important role in communication, especially prior to the rut.

These signposts are more popularly referred to as "buck rubs" and "scrapes". Although rubs are made with the antlers, they are also probably marked with secretions from the buck's forehead glands. Scrapes are pawed areas in the soil which include urine deposits as well as scent-marking of overhead tree branches probably with secretions from the forehead, preorbital and nasal glands as well as saliva.

Most signposting is done by mature bucks, presumably to advertise their dominance, individual identity, and other information of social importance. Researchers Larry Marchinton and Karl Miller propose that primer pheromones deposited by dominant bucks — especially during the pre-rut period — at rubs and scrapes help synchronize reproductive cycles, bring adult does into estrus early, and suppress the aggressiveness and sex drive of young bucks.

Compared to older bucks, yearling bucks are more delayed physiologically and psychologically in entering rut condition. Most yearlings are generally delayed a week or two in shedding antler velvet and never do achieve the sex hormone "highs" that stimulate mature bucks.

As a result, these younger bucks, on average, only make about one-half as many rubs and 15 percent as many scrapes as older bucks. Since yearlings make very few rubs during the early pre-rut, an abundance of antler rubs during September and early October invariably reveal the presence of a dominant buck 3.5 years of age or older.

While scraping behavior among whitetail bucks is done instinctively, it is a trait that improves with practice and experience. Mature bucks tend to scent-mark overhead limbs year round, but normally do not develop full-fledged scrapes by pawing the ground beneath the limbs until early September. Yearling bucks tend to commence scraping about six weeks later than mature bucks.

The overhead limb is an essential part of the scrape. Without it, there is no scrape. If you take away the limb, the most traditional, diligently pawed scrape will disappear. On the other hand, if you add a limb in the right location, bucks will paw the turf beneath it with dedication, forming a new scrape where none had ever existed — without further human doctoring of the site.

Regardless of their age, whitetail bucks exhibit peak scraping activity at about the time the first does breed — during the last week of October or first week of November. The important thing to note is that most scraping activity (50 percent to 60 percent) occurs before the first doe breeds, and the frequency of new scrapes declines sharply thereafter.

On average, prime-age bucks only freshen and maintain slightly more than half of the scrapes they make, versus about a 40 percent re-treatment rate for yearling bucks. Due to their more frequent re-pawing of scrapes, prime-age bucks also tend to make larger scrapes than do younger bucks.

CONCLUSIONS

Antler velvet stripping, starting about the first of September, signals start of a seven- to eight-week chaotic period commonly referred to as the whitetail pre-rut. Although initially rather mild mannered and not very active, bucks simply go berserk in mid-October and for several weeks are more active than they are at any other time during the year.

All things considered, if I had my druthers, I'd be hunting during the last week of October and the first week of November, annually — when bucks are active about 80 percent of the time. ■

SECTION 2: RUT

chapter 10

CLIMBING THE SOUTHERN PEAKS

BOB HUMPHREY

▶ THROUGHOUT MUCH OF THE WHITETAIL'S range, the rut is a fairly synchronous event, occurring roughly about early to mid-November. As you move south, things change — sometimes dramatically.

In his book *Hunting Whitetails by the Moon*, Charles Alsheimer wrote, "In some parts of the South, nothing makes sense when predicting the rut." There are numerous mitigating factors, including climate, genetics, nutrition, sex ratio and radically different day lengths.

One of the biggest confounding factors involves adaptive strategies. Natural selection has programmed Northern deer to breed within a fairly narrow window. Their fawns must be born late enough so there's enough available food for nursing mothers and early enough that fawns can mature enough to survive their first winter. That's not so important for deer in the South, where spring comes early and winters are less severe.

Genetics is another related factor. Many parts of the South were restocked with Northern deer. Their genetic hard-wiring is still tuned into Northern day-length conditions. Mixing those deer with Southern genetic lines has resulted in intermediate breeding dates across the fall calendar.

Research has also shown that herd health has an influence. Dense herds and highly skewed sex and age ratios can throw off the rut's timing.

Fortunately, biologists keep pretty close tabs on peak breeding dates in their respective states. They do so in several ways, including measuring fetuses. From that, they can back-date to the conception date. The more data they collect, the more accurate their indices. What they find is a fair amount of variability, even within states.

This article summarizes what we know about peak breeding and rut dates from Southern states.

First, however, we must differentiate between peak rut and peak breeding. The rut encompasses all activity associated with breeding. This includes courtship rituals such as making and tending scrapes, seeking and chasing does, and sorting out male dominance through sparring and fighting. The peak rut is when all these activities are at their most intense, and bucks are most active and observable during daylight. Peak breeding is when the most does stand for a buck. The pair often seeks a secluded area and remains relatively sedate for a 12- to 24-hour period. Though there is considerable overlap, you can usually figure peak rut will occur about 10 days to two weeks before peak breeding.

COUNTRY ROAD, TAKE ME HOME

In Virginia, the rut is fairly typical of much of the northern part of the whitetail's range. Virginia deer project coordinator Matt Knox puts peak breeding just after mid-November through most of the state, possibly a little earlier moving east. Conception data collected by the state also indicates most adult does are bred during a six- to eight-day period.

In West Virginia, Chris Ryan, supervisor of game management services, said peak rutting activity in his state occurs roughly from Nov. 8 through Nov. 14, with some slight variation from north to south, and peak breeding occurring slightly later. As you move south, things begin to change.

CAROLINA ON MY MIND

Peak rut dates in North Carolina vary by more than a month on a geographical gradient. According to biologist Evin Stanford, the first peak occurs in the Lower Coastal Plain about Oct. 25. The Upper Coast Plain rut peaks about a week later, around Nov. 1. The Piedmont region has what you might consider a more typical mid-November peak. The Foothills rut peaks a week later, Nov. 21, and rut activity in the Mountains hits its apex at month's end.

South Carolina is slightly different. According to deer and turkey program coordinator Charles Ruth, the rut there also spans a month, with breeding from mid-

October to mid-November through much of the state. According to his data, about 80 percent of does conceive between Oct. 6 to Nov. 16. I've hunted the alleged mid-October peak in the Low Country but didn't see much in the way of rutting activity. Ruth refined his window by noting that the last week in October and the first week in November represent peak breeding, with Oct. 30 being the peak conception date. However, he cautioned that breeding chronology occurs on a bell-shaped curve.

THE BELL-SHAPED CURVE

South Carolina deer biologist Charles Ruth emphasized that when plotted on a graph, the distribution of breeding dates occurs on a bell shape around the average. Most does will be bred within a narrow period, with a decreasing number breeding before and after. The more synchronous the breeding, the higher and tighter the curve.

The level of synchrony is often related to herd health, with healthier herds — those with good sex and age ratios and in line with carrying capacity — having more synchronous and often more intense ruts.

EAT A PEACH

Georgia has an unusual range of peak breeding dates, which deer project coordinator Charlie Killmaster attributes at least partly to the warmer climate and deer restocking efforts. Hunters willing to travel in-state can enjoy peak rut from mid October to late January.

One such hunter is the Quality Deer Management Association Executive Director Brian Murphy. He's hunted four peaks in one season within his home state. Murphy said peak rut occurs about the second week of October in the coastal counties, followed by a mid-November rut across the bulk of the state. Peak in the northern 15 counties occurs a week later, about Nov. 20, with peak in the extreme southwestern portion of the state coming almost a month later, in mid-December.

GOING DOWN TO FLORIDA

When it comes to rut dates, Florida is the exception to the exception. According to biologist Tony Young, does in extreme southern Florida might enter estrus as

early as late July. At the opposite end of the spectrum is northwestern Florida (and some west-central areas), where the mean rut can be as late as early to mid-February. I've witnessed hard-horned bucks intently chasing does in mid-March. Rut dates between vary enough that you should probably consult a local source for accurate information.

SWEET HOME ALABAMA

Alabama biologist Chris Cook also described his state's peak breeding dates as highly variable, spanning from about Christmas to the first week of February. The difference occurs on somewhat of a north-to-south gradient, with deer in the state's northern half breeding from Christmas until mid-January, and those in the southern half typically breeding from mid-January to the first week of February. I try to time my annual sojourn to the Black Belt region for peak rut around the third week in January. Cook also said there are some areas with late-November breeding and others with early- to mid-December breeding.

MISSISSIPPI ON MY MIND

The Mississippi Department of Wildlife, Fisheries and Parks actually has a map on its website showing mean conception dates for the state. They progress in a roughly northwest-to-southeast direction, beginning in early December and ending in early February. Biologist Chad Daucus said hunters should remember that hunter-observable rutting activity peaks about two weeks before the mean breeding date.

DOWN SOUTH IN NEW ORLEANS

According to biologist Scott Durham, Louisiana deer breed from September to February. The Louisiana Department of Wildlife and Fisheries also prepared a map of peek breeding dates. Rather than a clean north-to-south gradient, however, dates vary depending on the area, habitat and herd parameters. Breeding peaks in late October in southwestern Louisiana and late November in much of the northwestern portion of the state. There's a late-December peak in the southeastern and north-central regions and in pockets of the northwestern part of the state. The last peak, in late January, occurs in a band roughly along the state's eastern fringe. As in other states, hunters should remember there might be considerable variability and overlap along the margins of peak rut bands.

THE REST

Kentucky's Lee McClellan said his state's rut occurs the middle two weeks of November, with the peak coming a few days to a week earlier in western Kentucky.

Daryl Ratajczak in Tennessee said his state's average conception dates vary slightly across the state, peaking Nov. 21 in the western part, Nov. 25 in the eastern portion and Nov. 17 in the two central regions.

Meanwhile, Brad Miller said Arkansas' statewide mean conception date is Nov. 18, give or take a week.

WE CAN'T FORGET ABOUT TEXAS

We couldn't do a comprehensive compendium of Southern rut dates without including Texas, particularly as deer researchers have already done such a good job of identifying intra-state variation in the Lone Star State. Here's a look at how it breaks down for this year:

PEAK BREEDING DATES FOR TEXAS

REGION	DATE
Gulf Prairies and Marshes	
northern	Sept. 30
southern	Oct. 31
Post Oak Savannah	Nov. 10
Pineywoods	
southern	Nov. 12
northern	Nov. 22
Cross Timbers	Nov. 15 to 17
Rolling Plains	
south	Nov. 20
north	Dec. 3
Edwards Plateau	
east	Nov. 7
central	Nov. 24
west	Dec. 5
Trans-Pecos	Dec. 8
Southern Texas Plains	
east	Dec. 16
west	Dec. 24

CONCLUSION

Numerous theories exist on what triggers the rut and when it occurs. Although the contrary theories have not necessarily been disproved, state agency biologists and all peer-reviewed research seem to agree on one. Though the specific dates might vary considerably from one state to another — and even within some states — peak rut and breeding dates do not vary from year to year.

Again, it's important to distinguish between peak rut and peak breeding dates, which might be as much as two weeks apart. You should also keep in mind that factors such as weather and temperature won't affect timing but can influence what you observe. If it's warm, deer will just move more at night. ■

chapter 11

WHY BIG BUCKS MOVE IN NASTY WEATHER

JOHN EBERHART

▶ IN AREAS WITH HEAVY CONSEQUENTIAL hunting pressure, foul weather can be your ace in the hole.

The mention of nasty weather makes many bowhunters reconsider their hunting plans. Depending on its severity, rain, wind, cold or snow can make hunting miserable. So, during severe weather, most bowhunters stay out of the woods. That's unfortunate, because they might be missing some great opportunities, especially in areas with heavy consequential hunting pressure.

I hunt in nasty weather, but not because I enjoy being miserable or want to risk getting sick. My motivation is very clear and self-centered. Mature bucks in areas with heavy consequential hunting pressure seem to feel more comfortable moving during inclement weather than during bluebird conditions. This fact has been pounded home through years of hunting and observation in such areas.

PRESSURE AND WEATHER

There's likely a study somewhere supporting my observations, but although studies are nice, I know of none from areas with heavy consequential hunting pressure, so they mean nothing to me. Not all deer grow up equally. Some inhabit areas that see tremendous consequential hunting pressure, where nearly every hunter is targeting any legal antlered buck. Others live in areas with little or no hunting pressure or properties with hunter engagement rules. Heavy consequential hunting pressure has an effect on deer behavior and daytime movement habits.

Let's be honest: Most TV or video personalities hunt on managed leases or ranches, or in areas with extremely low hunter densities. In such areas, there is no need to hunt in foul weather to take big bucks. These spots hold many mature bucks, and they move during mornings and evenings just like other deer, no matter the conditions. I speak from direct experience, having hunted public land for 47 years in the state that annually has the most bowhunters in the country, and having taken 16 one-week out-of-state hunts to lightly hunted states. The daytime movement habits of the few bucks that survive to maturity in areas with heavy consequential hunting pressure are staggeringly different than those of the many mature bucks in managed and lightly hunted areas.

So what do heavily hunted bucks like about foul weather? They obviously can't go inside, so it makes no difference whether they're bedded or up and moving. Or maybe it's their ability to move in silence. Ever notice how cautiously mature deer move during dry, calm conditions, taking a few steps and stopping to listen for any possible reaction to their movement? Only mature deer know whether buck movement during nasty weather is a natural phenomenon or whether it's because they have not encountered hunters on such days. I think it's likely a combination of previous survival history and the ability to move in silence. Any time there's a lack of consequences for actions, those actions will likely be repeated.

My hunting log backs up this theory with big buck sightings and kills. In the late 1960s and early 1970s, I noticed that mature deer movements increased during inclement weather. Every December around Christmas, I'd travel with a couple of friends to northern Michigan to bowhunt public land. During snowstorms, high winds and brutal cold, buck movements would escalate far beyond that of nice days. It became clear that pressured mature bucks move more in daylight during inclement weather.

RAINY CONDITIONS

My records show that almost 40 percent of my mature buck sightings in Michigan occurred during inclement weather, generally during periods of light to moderate precipitation. This is an extraordinary percentage when you consider that less than 15 percent of my hunts occur during those conditions. At age 60, I now struggle with hunting during inclement weather, but I still go out of my way to do so. That's exactly the opposite of what most hunters do, which fits my typical thought process when hunting heavy consequential hunting pressure areas.

During rain, it's critical to take only short broadside shots, in which the likelihood of the arrow passing through both lungs is high. Double-lung-hit deer rarely travel farther than 100 yards before dying and should be easily recovered, even with a poor or totally washed-out blood trail. That should be everyone's mantra in the first place, but unfortunately, it isn't always the case. The last thing you want to do during rain is take a marginal shot, make a marginal hit and lose the deer because the blood washed away.

During a 2004 hunt, I sat from daylight to dark in gut-wrenching rain for three consecutive days. I had seen a huge buck during my first scouting day and wanted him pretty bad. When the alarm went off at 3 a.m. on the fourth morning, it was still raining, and my stamina was waning, to say the least. I considered shutting off the alarm and going back to sleep, but thank God I didn't. Just after daybreak, the buck I had been waiting for busted out of nearby stranding corn in pursuit of a doe and made a bad decision to stop broadside 25 yards away. His mishap cost him his life, as I slid an arrow through both lungs, watched him run 80 yards and die. My previous inconveniences were immediately warranted.

Hunting in the rain used to be an act of suffering. PVC-lined Nylon-exterior rainsuits were stiff and loud, and I always opted to get wet rather than wear them. During a steady downpour in 1977, I took a good buck while being soaked to the bone. The

next season from the same tree, I took another decent buck in 30 mph winds.

Raingear for bowhunting must fulfill several criteria. It has to keep you dry, must be quiet, should allow ease of movement and should be somewhat durable.

In the early 1990s, garments with brushed polyester micro-fabric exteriors and waterproof Teflon and or polyurethane membranes became popular, and the marketplace is still saturated with similar garments. These membranes are noisy, and the short napped exterior micro-fleece doesn't mask the membrane noise very well. Short napped micro-fabric exteriors are also not very durable.

Browning's deep-napped Hydro-Fleece was the first waterproof clothing that, in my opinion, was quiet enough to bowhunt in, and it was very durable. Browning eventually abandoned the quiet Hydro-Fleece fabric and went to Hydro-Suede (short-napped micro fabric).

The quiet waterproof garment market remained what I considered stagnant until the early 2000s, when Rivers West came out with a dense, deep-napped fleece fabric that masked the noise of the membrane. The company called it H2P. Rivers West garments have made it possible to remain dry and hunt comfortably in downright deluges. They are also extremely durable.

The words waterproof and breathable should never be used in the same sentence, let alone next to each other. The tests used for breathability in the hunting industry are rather meaningless. They are simple vapor transfer tests that practically any materials other than rubber or cellophane could pass.

Garments labeled as waterproof/breathable lack air permeability, which is why they can also be used as windproof garments during cold, windy days. To test that concept, I took a brand-name non-insulated "waterproof/breathable"-labeled jacket and draped it over a large fan. I turned the fan on high and then lit a match on the opposite side. The flame never flickered. Reversing the jacket over the fan produced the same results. There are no waterproof suits through which you can blow air from either side. Garments are waterproof or breathable (permeable), but they cannot be both.

Any meaningful breathability of a waterproof suit can only come through venting, which requires visible openings that allow air flow. Some garments accomplish that with zippered openings and mesh panels with covered flaps.

WINDY CONDITIONS

For decades, strong winds had me baffled, and that's still my least preferred condition in which to hunt. Unlike a light drizzle or rain, in which a deer's senses are not diminished, heavy wind causes problems for deer. Heavy winds make noise, produce lots of movement in the woods and swirl scent in unpredictable directions. With all three of their main defenses against predators impaired, it's obvious why deer don't move as well in heavy wind as during other conditions.

Although mature bucks in areas with heavy consequential hunting pressure often move during extremely windy conditions, other deer usually move less than normal. However, there's frequently a lull in the wind in the evening and morning. How many times have you decided not to hunt because of heavy wind only to have it stop about a half-hour before dark? As soon as the wind stops, the general deer traffic picks up, often with a determination not seen otherwise. Deer seem to know they have a window of time in which their sensory defenses will work before the wind increases again.

During high winds, your chances are diminished, but anything can happen. Like hunting in the rain and cold, hunting in the wind sometimes becomes a matter of attrition. Stick it out, and something good might happen. Or stay home, and assume nothing would have.

Proper clothing during cold, windy conditions is an absolute must. It doesn't matter how many layers of insulated undergarments you wear. If your exterior or first layer under that doesn't block the wind, the breeze will penetrate through your permeable insulation within a brief period and freeze you out. My choice of clothing is again Rivers West H2P fabric Ambush Jacket and Trail Pants as exterior garments during extremely cold, windy conditions, with an activated carbon Scent-Lok garment as my first layer beneath it.

Just as with rain, you need to shorten your shot distances during windy conditions, because wind can and usually will cause erratic arrow flight and affect accuracy more than rain, especially if it's a stiff cross wind.

In 2000, I took my most prized Michigan buck during a severely windy afternoon. About an hour after I set up, I almost fell out of my tree when the buck stood up in some nearby red willows not 40-yards from me and walked within shooting range. Had it not been windy, there's no doubt he would have heard my approach or ascent into the tree and spooked.

COLD AND SNOWY CONDITIONS

Hunting during a snowfall is similar to rain. Light to moderate snow, basically a frozen drizzle, seems to be best. Just as during rain, mature bucks will likely be on their feet in these conditions for the same reasons. The upside of hunting in snow is that current deer sign is obvious.

In mid-October 1996, during a torrential downpour, I went out to prepare a new location. By noon, I was drenched but finished. During my exit along a standing cornfield, I encountered the big buck I was pursuing working a scrape in the still-pouring rain. We made immediate eye contact, and after a few stare-down seconds, the buck bolted into the nearby woods. I saw that buck only three times in four sea-

sons, and it was raining during two of those encounters. In November 1997, I took that buck at noon soon after it had just stopped snowing.

Deer don't move much during extremely high winds and cold weather because the cold winds penetrate their coats and makes them use more energy. They usually bed in low areas or dense conifers, both of which provide protection from the wind. But sometimes, bucks move, and that's enough for me.

On public land two days after gun season ended in 2008, I took a big buck during blizzard conditions. It was 7 degrees and snowing hard, with steady 30- to 40-mph winds. I saw five bucks during the last half-hour of light, and I nearly got out of my tree before that because I couldn't imagine anything other than my stupid self moving in those conditions.

There 's always one solid guarantee: If you're not out there, you can't kill anything.

In areas with heavy consequential hunting pressure, a mature buck's only point of vulnerability might be during nasty weather. So if you're suitably prepared and have the desire, get out there and hunt. After all, what else is there to do? ■

chapter 12

WHITETAIL JET FUEL:
HOW TESTOSTERONE CONTROLS THE RUT

CHARLES J. ALSHEIMER

▶ I'VE BEEN INTERESTED IN WHITETAIL behavior for more than five decades. As a teenage hunter, I had many questions about why bucks and does do what they do and look the way they look at various times of year. As I progressed through life as a hunter, photographer and writer, many of those questions were answered. However, it wasn't until I began raising whitetails more than 20 years ago that my understanding of them went to the next level, especially when it came to rutting behavior.

Each year, hundreds of articles are written explaining why bucks throw caution to the wind, expand their home ranges, rub, scrape, fight, chase and breed. Though rutting behavior is fascinating, I believe few hunters truly know what drives a buck to do what he does during the rut.

There isn't one aspect of rut behavior that stands on its own merits. Rather, all are part of a recipe driven by environmental factors and hormones. Everything leading up to breeding happens for a reason and has a purpose. To understand the whitetail's journey to the rut requires an understanding of how whitetails exist 365 days a year.

PHOTO PERIOD AND HORMONES

The process of photoperiodism is responsible for the seasonal and behavioral changes we witness in the natural world; everything from bird migrations to season changes. In the whitetail's case, when the vernal equinox leaves winter behind, day length begins to increase rapidly. This triggers many physical changes in whitetails,

one of which is the shedding of winter fur. In addition, spring green-up brings an explosion in the quantity and quality of food available to deer. But the most noticeable change in whitetails in spring and summer is the effect lengthening daylight has on antler growth. Though it is believed hormones have a role in antler growth, a deer's health and day length are the big drivers.

From January to mid-August, a buck's testicular volume and serum testosterone levels are low. By late August, shortening day length becomes more noticeable, triggering an uptick in hormones in bucks and does. For bucks, the testosterone increase is slow at first because nature is careful not to give them their full arsenal of rutting behaviors until the time is right.

Between mid-August and mid-September, a buck's testosterone level will increase nearly 100 percent from what it was in June. And from mid-September to Nov. 1, it will double again, reaching its peak by the first week in November in the North. A doe's estrogen level will also peak around Nov. 1, setting the stage for breeding to occur. Here in western New York, velvet peel is full-blown around Sept. 1. From that point on, rut behaviors begin increasing until reaching their apex in November.

PHYSICAL CHANGE

Throughout summer, the physical appearance of bucks is noticeably different from what it will be in November. Because their testosterone is low in summer, the bodies of bucks will be sleek and slender, particularly in the neck. With little testosterone to drive aggressive tendencies, bucks assimilate into bachelor groups throughout summer, bedding together, feeding at the same food sources and often grooming each other. However, by the time velvet-clad antlers are ready to peel, testosterone begins to flow. When velvet peel has occurred, bucks begin to spar with each other. With each passing day, the testosterone valve opens a little more, and with it comes the first signs of rutting behavior. By mid-September, a Northern buck's winter fur is nearly grown in, and his body begins to fill out. In some mature bucks, this increase in body mass almost gives the impression that the buck is being blown up with an air hose.

In human terms, the effects that testosterone therapy has on athletes is well documented and rivals what occurs with whitetail bucks when their testosterone level increases. For example, when a human male athlete undergoes testosterone therapy, his muscle mass begins to increase, especially if he is involved in a weight-training program. In addition, an athlete's muscle twitch greatly improves, meaning his reaction time is quicker, and he can run faster. During the 1990s, many baseball players began taking performance-enhancing drugs (primarily testosterone) to boost performance. Players who normally hit 20 to 25 home runs a year were hitting 40 and 50. In the process, home run records that had stood for decades were shattered. Fortunately, Major League Baseball took steps to rid the sport of performance-enhancing drugs, but some players continue to cheat the system. Though steroid use helped records fall, the dirty little secret is that there is a dark side to improper steroid use. Side effects can include making an athlete hyper-active and very aggressive, in some instances dangerous to themselves and others.

I share the baseball comparison to say this: In all my years of raising whitetails, I've witnessed very similar behavioral traits and patterns in bucks when their hormones increase unabated. From mid-December to mid-September, when testosterone levels are low, Northern bucks bed a great deal, for the most part keep to themselves and show little aggression to other deer in their home ranges. However, when

September begins inching toward November and hormone levels increase and peak, bucks turn into different creatures.

PHYSICAL AND BEHAVIORAL EFFECTS

Body: The first noticeable effect elevated testosterone has on bucks occurs soon after velvet peel, when the neck size of bucks begins to increase. To illustrate this, I've included two photos I took of an Ohio buck. The first shows him soon after antler peel in early September. The second was taken in early November. This physical change is quite typical, especially for mature bucks, and I believe it's a necessary process bucks go through to determine dominance.

Attitude: Increased levels of testosterone transform a buck from being docile from January through September to almost being a mad man by the time the rut explodes. When a buck's testosterone valve is fully opened, no deer in his home range is safe. Therefore, few bucks come out of the rut without wounds. In some cases, they are so intoxicated with testosterone that their temper gets them killed.

Fighting: By mid-August, a buck's testosterone level has increased to the point that the buck starts to show aggression toward other bucks in its bachelor group. From this point to velvet peel, stare-downs and threat-walking — precursors to fighting — are common. Twice, I've seen bucks aggressively fight antler to antler in full velvet during the week before velvet peel.

After velvet peel occurs, a buck's attitude changes for the worse. Throughout September, much sparring occurs, and when October arrives, sparring matches can become quite ugly. From late October through early December, when testosterone levels are highest, fight-to-the-death encounters are common.

Activity: Testosterone levels greatly affect a buck's activity level. To use a human example, testosterone does to bucks what amphetamines do to humans. During summer, when testosterone levels are low, bucks move very little, and it's not uncommon for their home range to be less than 400 acres before

mid-September. However, as soon as a buck's testosterone valve is opened, a buck beds less and moves much more. Research has shown that by Oct. 1, a buck's home range can be four to five times what it was in August.

When testosterone peaks in early November, a buck can easily cover more than 4,000 acres. When this happens, he encounters bucks he's never seen before. As a result, fighting becomes the norm, and nothing good comes from these encounters.

Rubbing: When velvet peel occurs, there seems to be a lull in rubbing behavior, until about Oct. 1 in the North. From that point, rubbing intensifies before dropping off when breeding is finished. It's well known that most of the rubbing done by bucks is for scent marking. However, I believe the most intense rubbing occurs because of the high level of testosterone in a buck's system in October and November. When testosterone levels decrease, rubbing also drops off.

Scraping: Whitetails (bucks and does) will work overhanging licking branches 365 days a year to scent-mark their territories. It's their way of communicating with all deer in their home range. Through the years, I've studied the whitetail's scraping behavior extensively and observed that it doesn't become intense until testosterone levels are near peak. In my area of New York state, scraping starts to explode about Oct. 15 each year before dropping off when the breeding period becomes full-blown.

A part of the scraping process is rub-urination. During the final step of making a scrape, a buck brings his tarsal glands together and urinates through them as he rubs them together. Though I've photographed this behavior every month, it doesn't reach its peak until testosterone levels peak in early November in the North.

Doe etiquette: Without elevated testosterone levels, bucks pretty much leave does alone. With elevated testosterone, it's, "Katy bar the door," especially in the two-week period before peak breeding. During the two weeks leading up to breeding, bucks are relentless in their pursuit of does. Chasing can be intense, and if a buck corners a does in a blow-down or thick brush, the doe can be injured.

Breeding: As mentioned, testosterone and testicular volume in a buck and estrogen in a doe peak around the Nov. 1 in the North. This synchronization sets the stage for breeding to occur. Though testosterone drives the breeding process, high levels of the hormone are not required for a buck to breed a doe. Twice in my years of raising whitetails, I've seen antlerless bucks (they had shed their antlers in early February) attempt to breed does that cycled into estrus in March. Because of the bucks' physical appearance, I knew their testosterone levels had bottomed out, but the smell of estrus still drove them to breed.

CONCLUSION

For more than five decades, I've been immersed in the whitetail's world. Though I love photographing them every month of the year, nothing gets my whitetail juices flowing faster than thoughts of hunting or photographing during the rut. I find all aspects of their rutting behavior intriguing and energizing, and I feel blessed to have witnessed their world as I have.

Many things go into making whitetail behavior so fascinating. If I've learned one thing, it is this: Without the effects of hormones, autumn in the whitetail's world would not be the same. Just as it takes gas to run a car, it takes testosterone to fuel a rutting buck. ■

chapter 13

WHO RULES THE RUT?

CHARLES J. ALSHEIMER

▶ ALMOST 10 DAYS HAD PASSED since the November full moon hung full in the sky. The rut was hot to trot, and with the smell of does floating on the wind, the mature 10-pointer's mission was finding a doe to breed.

A cold, steady breeze blew from the northwest. With a mixture of rain and snow falling, the buck emerged from a standing cornfield. Cautiously, he entered a woods that descended into a deep ravine and paused to assess the surroundings. Below in a tangle of treetops and second growth, he heard the faint sound of a deer snorting. Hurriedly, he walked toward the sound. When he reached the rim of the ravine, he heard deer running. He picked up the pace and dropped into the ravine for a closer look. Halfway down the steep incline, he solved the mystery. A breeding party was in progress.

At the bottom of the ravine, the 10-pointer encountered several deer scattered among a thick tangle of blowdowns along a trickling stream. A yearling buck and two fawns were milling around a doe that was standing in a cluster of low-growing hemlock saplings just above the stream bed. As the big buck approached, the doe turned to look into the thick brush that bordered the creek. The 10-pointer paused, sensing another deer was nearby. Just then, an impressive 3½-year-old 9-pointer came into view, trotting toward the doe. The doe bolted and ran for a tangle of treetops upstream and bedded.

Before the 9-pointer could get to the doe, the mature 10-pointer charged. Both bucks came to a halt and stared at each other. The 10-pointer let out a loud, extended wheeze as the 9-pointer shifted his gaze back and forth between the big buck and the doe. Neither buck was about to back down.

The bucks lunged at each other, and their antlers came together, making a loud clacking sound. The woods was now a war zone. First, the 10-pointer and then the 9-pointer gained the advantage as they pushed each other back and forth. Periodically, they unlocked and relocked their antlers, after which they would resume pushing. Throughout the ordeal, small saplings in their path were flattened or ripped from the ground. The sound of antlers clacking together, branches breaking, and moaning and grunting could be heard for a long distance. It was a fight to behold.

In little more than a minute, the bucks were exhausted. They were panting so hard that steam shot from their mouths when they exhaled. With their antlers locked, the 9-pointer gained an advantage when he pushed the 10-pointer against a fallen log. The force caused their antlers to unlock. Before the 10-pointer could regain his balance, the 9-pointer rammed his antlers into the mature buck's side. At the impact, the 10-pointer let out a loud moan. Before the sound faded, the 9-pointer rammed his rack into the older buck's flank. The force prompted the 10-pointer to spring to his feet and half-stumble, half-run through the woods. The fight was finished.

For the next hour, the 9-pointer stood awkwardly in the forest, trying to recover from the fight. Steam shot from his mouth and nostrils with every breath. He couldn't stop panting. When nightfall swallowed the forest, the 9-pointer had recovered enough to look for the doe that was responsible for what he had gone through. When he found her less than 100 yards away, he bedded nearby.

IT'S NOT ALWAYS ABOUT AGE

As a hunter and photographer I've witnessed scenes like that many times. At seminars, I'm often asked which age class drives the rut's intensity. My answer often surprises people, because most believe that it takes bucks 4½ or older to have a truly intense rut. Before sharing an opinion on this, let me offer some background and observations.

For starters I've been blessed to have hunted whitetails in some of the most incredible locations in North America. For more than 40 of those years, I've passionately pursued whitetails with a camera when I'm not hunting them with guns and bow and arrows. And during the past 20 years, I've had the eye-opening experience of raising them for behavioral study. No, I don't know all there is about white-tailed deer, but I've seen a lot in my half century of chasing them.

So, when someone asks which age class of bucks drives the rut's intensity, I begin by asking where they live and what kind of management program exists in their area. Though attitudes and management practices are changing, it's safe to say that in more than 75 percent of the whitetail's range, there are no age or antler restrictions in place to let bucks reach maturity. Consequently, for most of America, the rut's intensity is driven by yearling bucks, because bucks older than 2½ are few and far between. For example, here in western New York, more than 70 percent of the antlered buck harvest is made up of yearlings.

However, if the age structure of a deer herd could be evenly represented from age 1 to 7, you might be surprised by which age class is most responsible for driving the rut's intensity.

AGE/BEHAVIOR

Having raised many white-tailed bucks from birth to death, I've witnessed firsthand how they mature. If a buck can remain healthy, it's possible for him to live 10 to 12 years. Because of that, they progress through life much the same way as human males (who live to be 75 years on average). As a result, it's easy to match a whitetail's life cycle with that of a human.

1½-year-old buck: This age class is very similar to pre-teen boys. When bucks reach this age and get their first surge of testosterone, they start paying attention to does. They are also trying to figure out what life is all about. If older bucks are not common in their home range, they will do most of the breeding. Because every buck has a different personality, rutting attitudes will vary greatly within this age class. If older bucks are common, this age class will exhibit little rutting behavior.

2½-year-old buck: This age class is comparable to a 14- to 16-year-old human male. Though far from being mature, this age class will drive the rut's intensity in most deer herds because of a lack of older bucks. Though still a work in progress, a buck of this age class knows what the rut is all about.

3½-year-old buck: Bucks in this age class are studs, similar to 17- to 20-year-old men. At 3, the skeletal frame of a buck is complete, though muscle mass will be added as he ages. When a buck turns 3, he's a true athlete, and most bucks of this age have an attitude to match.

4½-year-old buck: This guy is very similar to a 21- to 26-year-old man who believes he has things figured out. Most have a chip on their shoulder, meaning they have a bad attitude when it comes to interacting with other bucks during the rut. In well-managed deer herds, where all age classes are present, a 4½-year-old will be a dominant breeder.

5½- to 7½-year-old buck: This is my favorite age class. Age-wise, they are very similar to men 27 to 45 years old. They are in the prime of life and have antlers that can be beyond impressive. They also have a tendency to be nocturnal, with a home range smaller than those of 3½- and 4½-year-olds.

8½- to 9½-year-old buck: Few hunters have ever seen a free-ranging buck in this category because they do not exist, except in rare cases. Bucks in this age class are equivalent to 46- to 59-year-old men. Because of injuries, few in this age class make it past bullets, arrows, coyotes, wolves and, in the North, severe winter conditions.

If a buck reaches this age, he will still deposit scent by scraping and rubbing, but he will mostly do a limited amount of breeding if there are 3½- to 7½-year-old bucks in the deer herd. For the most part, 8- and 9-year-old bucks are totally nocturnal.

10½- to 12½-year-old buck: I've never seen a buck this old in the wild, but I've raised a bunch. If you could see a whitetail buck this old, you'd say, "Wow, he's an old man." That he is, because his attitude and physical traits rival that of a 60-year-old man. Can he still breed? Yes. Does he? Not if younger bucks are in the population. At this age, bucks are usually gaunt looking, with antler size decreasing significantly from 10 to 12. Most bucks in this age group are loners and nocturnal.

WHO DRIVES THE BUS?

If you picked up what occurred in the opening of this article, you will have noticed that the 3½-year-old buck took the doe from the mature 10-pointer. After a lifetime of pursuing and taking more than 1 million photos of whitetails, I believe the driver of the whitetail rut is the 3½-year-old age class. My reasons are many.

If there are older bucks in the herd, most 3½-year-old bucks will not have been injured previously because they were intimidated by older bucks when they were yearlings and 2½-year-olds. So, they are healthy. Also, bucks of that age are incredible athletes with overflowing energy to burn, making them true marathoners. By this age, their antlers can be impressive, and most living in the North will have a live weight of 185 to 220 pounds, so they are no longer threatened by older mature bucks. And their attitude resembles that of a pit bull ready to pounce. Couple that with the fact that every 3½-year-old buck has seen three previous ruts — when he was a fawn, 1½ and 2½ — and it's easy to see that this age class is ready to rumble. Simply put, these bucks are driven to be the breeders, and few will play second fiddle to any other buck, regardless of size or age. If a 3½-year-old loses a fight with another buck, he will simply move until he finds an area where he can be king of the hill.

I've been impressed by how far some of our area's 3½-year-old bucks travel when dominance is determined and the rut kicks in. During summer, it's not uncommon to see and capture on trail cameras 3½-year-old bachelor groups feeding together in my food plots. Then, when velvet peel occurs and the rut approaches, many disappear — some for extended periods — until the rut is over. Several landowners in my area use cameras, so we've documented not only where some of the bucks went but how far they went. It's not uncommon for these 3½-year-olds to travel more than two miles from where we photographed them before the rut.

Make no mistake, all white-tailed bucks have the urge to breed, but when it comes to the age class that creates the most rut-related commotion in the woods, my vote goes to the 3½-year-old buck. ■

chapter 14

ECLIPSING THE MOON THEORY

JEREMY FLINN, DR. BRONSON STRICKLAND, DR. STEVE DEMARAIS

▶HUMANS HAVE CONJURED UP SOME amazing theories through the years.

In the baby-making genre, some say you can predict a baby's gender based on mom's craving for spicy food. And, a 700-year old Chinese calendar predicts gender based on moon age at the time a woman gets pregnant and the lunar month in which a child was conceived. It's hard to believe that spice or the lunar age and month could affect your baby's gender.

Humans have also generated lots of theories about animal behavior based on celestial bodies, such as the moon. Obviously, because the moon's gravitational pull changes the tides, fish and other aquatic animals can be greatly affected. But what about land animals, specifically the most pursued game species in North America, the white-tailed deer?

Many theories suggest white-tailed deer activity and breeding season are influenced by the moon. Many hunters believe these theories so much they plan their hunting trips around the moon phase or positioning. In fact, millions of dollars are spent every year on moon-influenced products, such as calendars, books and even trail cameras with moon-phase stamping on photos.

There's a lot of marketing hype, but has scientific evidence ever supported these claims? Much white-tailed deer research often goes unnoticed by the public. Magazines and TV shows such as Deer & Deer Hunting, and organizations such as the Quality Deer Management Association bridge the gap between the scientific and hunting communities. However, most hunters would rather read about practical management on food plots, trail cameras and hunting strategies than DNA sequencing, disease implications and sex-age-kill models.

Still, hunters are always interested in anything that might boost their success, and there's been some high-tech research conducted on how the moon affects white-tailed deer activity and breeding.

DEER ACTIVITY AND MOON PHASE

Most claims that the moon affects deer activity revolve around the new and full moons. Several books and articles describing the theory state that during a full moon, more deer will feed or become more active at night. Conversely, when the moon is in the new phase, deer will be more active during daylight. Some folks have even claimed that mature bucks will move during midday when there is a new moon.

These claims examine moon illumination, distance to the moon and moon declination (position). Branching off this main theory, some folks believe deer activity is greatest when the moon is overhead or underfoot. Others have gone out on a limb to quantify the number of days to and from a specific moon phase when deer activity will be the highest.

With all this "lunar guidance" attempting to shed light on the mystery of deer activity, what does the science and research say?

Improved technology has answered many questions that plagued scientists for decades. GPS-based telemetry collars have let us document habitat preference when hunting pressure is high and home-range size of bucks during the rut. These collars on free-ranging (wild) deer can collect a location every few minutes. The highest-quality collars can even send the location coordinates back to the researcher in almost real time. So you can rest assure these theories have been examined intensely.

One of the most intense deer activity studies ever conducted was done by Mickey Hellickson during his tenure at the University of Georgia. Using motion-sensing collars (not GPS collars) on 43 southern Texas bucks, Hellickson and his colleagues looked to classify a data point for a deer as "inactive" (bedding or standing) or "active" (feeding, walking or running). Bucks were monitored 24 hours a day by technicians receiving activity signals from VHF (very high frequency) transmitters, allowing the researchers to determine if bucks move more at night during a full moon. With two years of data, Hellickson and his colleagues compared movement during four to five days around a full moon and four to five days around a new moon. They found there was no difference in buck activity between the phases.

Some people claim that Texas is its own world when it comes to whitetails, so we also looked at similar studies in other locations. Researchers from Southern Illinois University also concluded that moon phase had no effects on buck activity. However, a study from Maryland reported that some data indicated mature buck activity could be greater during dark moon phases in the pre-rut. Those results do not support or dismiss the theory that bucks are more active during daylight during the new moon (dark phase). Using trail camera photos, longtime Deer and Deer Hunting contributor Charles Alsheimer showed there was no relationship between moon position (overhead or underfoot) and deer activity at his New York property.

Scientific research indicates the moon does not affect deer activity, but could it affect the timing of breeding? This is the theory many hunters hang their vacation days on each year, so let's dive deep into it.

THE RUT AND MOON PHASE

Alsheimer, the most popular lunar theorist, claims that changes in moonlight affect melatonin levels, with ultimate effects on the timing of reproduction. He states that in the North (north of about the 35th latitude), when the second full moon after the Autumnal Equinox occurs between late October and Nov. 12, peak breeding will begin seven days after the full moon. When the second full moon after the Autumnal Equinox occurs Nov. 13 or later, peak breeding will begin on the full moon. You

might have read our previous articles on the rut in *Deer & Deer Hunting*. In those, we explained how the annual breeding cycle of bucks and does is regulated by photoperiod, which is simply the relative amount of daylight and darkness throughout the year. The amount of daylight is unconsciously perceived by deer through the optic nerve, which ultimately signals the brain to release specialized hormones. Here's an example of how powerfully photoperiod can influence deer, particularly bucks: When artificial light was used to manipulate the annual photoperiod cycle, captive bucks grew and shed four sets of antlers in a year. In other words, researchers condensed what would typically be a 12-month photoperiod cycle into three months, and the bucks responded accordingly.

In our rut articles, we discussed how much a doe's reproductive physiology determines when a buck will act "rutty." As with bucks, photoperiod triggers a cocktail of hormones within a doe that will lead her into estrus. She will then breed only when the right concentrations of hormones are present. If a doe does not conceive during her first estrous cycle, she will cycle again until she becomes pregnant. Research has shown this cycle can occur up to seven times in does.

So if photoperiod drives most physiological and behavioral changes in whitetails, how can the moon influence these processes — specifically the breeding season — from one year to the next? We believe, based on significant research across the country, that it does not. There are several factors other than photoperiod that have been shown to affect breeding dates.

Does exposed to higher-quality nutrition might breed earlier than those with poor nutrition. Research has shown does with higher amounts of fat — specifically kidney fat — bred earlier than does with less fat. Seeing how changes in quality of diet can alter peak breeding, it should be expected that significant habitat improvements, supplemental feeding and food plot additions could shift peak breeding dates earlier.

Another cause for change in peak breeding dates in a wild deer herd is the adult sex ratio, or buck-to-doe ratio. Whitetails are classified as a polygynous species, meaning one male will breed with many females, and the female will typically breed with only one male. This is mostly true, but the Mississippi State University Deer Ecology and Management Lab documented that does will actually breed with more than one buck. Genetic analysis of wild deer determined that about 25 percent of twin litters had different fathers. That means does were obviously breeding with more than one buck. In situations where there are not enough bucks to breed all the does in estrus, a doe will re-enter estrus 28 days later. If that occurs enough, the average peak breeding date will be pushed later from one year to the next because more does are not being bred until their second estrus cycle. This is often what hunters call the second rut. To prevent this from happening, and to facilitate a more intense rut the first time, more does should be harvested and bucks protected.

A few years ago, the MSU Deer Lab initiated a study to critically examine the potential influence of the moon on breeding dates of captive and free-range deer from Mississippi and Texas. Through the years, we and our colleagues from Texas have collected fawning dates for individual does, from which it was determined when each doe conceived (the date fawns were born minus the length of pregnancy equals the date bred). For each year, we compared the timing of the "rutting moon" with the observed breeding dates of the research does. We found the breeding dates did not correspond with the annual changes in the rutting moon. That is, the timing of the rutting moon changed, but the breeding dates did not change in a similar fashion. A similar study was conducted on 10 wild populations of deer in Mississippi. The results agreed with those from prior research.

In case you're thinking we're biased toward our own research, there have been several other studies showing similar results. The University of Georgia conducted a large-scale analysis — using data from Georgia, Mississippi, Texas, Missouri, Virginia, Maine, Michigan, Minnesota and South Carolina — comparing the effects of moon phase on breeding dates compared to that of photoperiod and weather. During the research period, the hunter's moon had an average change of more than 11 days and was highly variable. Researchers determined that photoperiod played a significant role and that breeding dates were relatively consistent within herds from year to year.

Hellickson and his colleagues also examined the predictability of the hunter's moon. Of the six years of breeding data they collected, only two, or 33 percent, fell within hunter's moon predictive period.

CONCLUSION

The bottom line is no studies support the theory that the moon affects deer activity or movement. Weather, hunting pressure and time of year will likely be the most driving factors for deer activity. Photoperiod, nutrition, genetics and adult buck-to-doe ratio are the driving forces of the breeding season

No matter what you believe, we'll leave you with two facts. First, whitetails are crepuscular, meaning they are most active at dusk and dawn. Last, no matter where you are in the whitetail's range, there are likely three weeks of fall during which you can't go wrong, and these will remain relatively consistent from one year to the next regardless of moon phase or position. ∎

chapter 15

BANG 'EM HARD DURING THE RUT

JOHN J. OZOGA

▶ WHEN I STARTED DEER HUNTING, nearly 60 years ago, my dad taught me to sit quietly. Back then, I couldn't even imagine creating a commotion by banging two pieces of bone together. And, I don't mind admitting, I have yet to kill my first buck using the antler rattling technique in upper Michigan, where forest cover is dense, deer populations are low, and mature bucks are not overly abundant.

The practice of antler rattling to attract whitetail bucks, by simulating buck sparring and fighting, apparently started in Texas during the early 1970s. Currently, it is widely used, presumably successfully, wherever deer are fairly abundant and populations have a reasonable adult sex ratio and buck age structure.

Popular literature abounds with stories of antler rattling success; so does advice relative to when and how to rattle in a big buck. Any hunter/writer who has drawn a buck into killing range via antler rattling immediately becomes a self-proclaimed deer calling expert, or so it seems. Unfortunately, antler rattling advice varies a great deal from one expert to the next. Scientific study of the subject appears quite limited.

SPARRING VS. FIGHTING

Antlers are unique structures found only among members of the deer family, Cervidae. They evolved hand-in-hand with certain aspects of breeding behavior.

Initially, soon after antler velvet stripping, bucks engage in "skill sparring." In skill sparring, a buck gains knowledge of the size of his antlers and how they relate to those of other bucks. They merely click their antlers together with minimal pushing and shoving. Even large-antlered bucks might tolerate such contact with smaller, younger bucks.

"Demonstrative sparring" is different. Even a friendly match of skill sparring might turn into a more decisive bout of demonstrative sparring. The purpose of these more serious encounters is to assess and establish social rank prior to the rut. Bucks push with all their might. This is a true test of physical strength. There is always a winner and a loser.

Violent "dominance fighting" is less common. True fights can lead to serious injury and even death. Such aggressive interactions tend to be brief and situational in nature. Usually, they occur only among evenly matched, prime-aged bucks during the rut, often in competition for an estrous female.

Generally, more fighting occurs when deer are abundant, when the adult sex ratio is closely balanced, and when a high proportion of bucks are 3.5 years or older. Combatants need not be strangers, and serious fighting might erupt anytime during the breeding season while male testosterone levels are high.

Logically, antler rattling is employed in hopes that it sounds like the real thing (i.e., two bucks sparring socially or fighting over possession of an estrous female) and results in attracting an inquisitive buck into killing range.

THE STUDY

Despite considerable study of whitetail breeding behavior, few studies have documented the effectiveness of antler rattling to attract bucks. In fact, I can find only one published scientific account designed to evaluate the role of antler rattling as a deer hunting technique.

Researchers from the Universities of Texas A&M and Georgia, led by Mickey Hellickson and Karl Miller, respectively, conducted two experiments to test whitetail buck response to antler rattling in Texas.

During one experiment, conducted on the Welder Wildlife Refuge from 1992-95, researchers determined buck response to four rattling sequences varying in duration and loudness. Generally, the observer was situated in an observation tower, while another performed the rattling upwind from a clump of brush.

Rattling sessions were performed during pre-rut, rut, and post-rut. All rut rattling sessions were conducted within one week of mean conception dates for the area (Nov. 22). Pre-rut and post-rut were then set as the one-month periods 15-45 days before and after the mean conception date. Responding bucks were videotaped and their ages were estimated by the observer.

A total of 171 rattling sessions resulted in attracting 111 bucks, 48 (43 percent) of which were observed at ground level.

The second experiment was conducted on the Faith Ranch, where researchers had previously attached activity-sensing radio transmitters to 48 bucks. Mean conception date for deer on the ranch was about a month later (Dec. 24) compared to deer on the Welder Refuge.

Radio-located bucks were approached to within 200 meters (downwind) before rattling. Then, each buck's response to rattling was monitored by telemetry. In all, 33 rattling sessions were performed near 18 radio-equipped bucks. If the radio signal indicated movement and became stronger, the buck was classified as having responded.

SEASONAL RESPONSE

In both experiments, total buck response to rattling was greatest during the rut and lowest during pre-rut. However, seasonal response rates varied according to buck age. That is, young bucks (1.5 and 2.5 years) were most responsive to rattling during the pre-rut period, whereas middle-aged bucks (3.5 and 4.5 years) more frequently responded during the rut.

Mature bucks (5.5 years and older) were slightly less responsive during peak-rut, possibly because they were already tending estrous females.

During post-rut, most young and middle-aged bucks had returned to traveling in bachelor groups. However, mature males were still testing females. These single, mature males represented the majority of responses to rattling during the post-rut.

This trend is undoubtedly related to seasonal variations in testosterone levels and mating opportunities. Peak sex hormone levels, which are achieved during the rut, contribute to increased fighting among older bucks. Logically, rattling is especially attractive to older bucks because it mimics competition for an estrous female.

The researchers found that single males observed from towers usually responded to rattling — "possibly because dominant males were not in the immediate area to discourage subordinates." On the other hand, young bucks probably are less likely to become involved in serious fights.

Conversely, increased sparring during the pre-rut and post-rut is associated with lower levels of testosterone. Also, bucks are more inclined to associate and travel in bachelor groups before and after the rut, increasing the likelihood of their coming into friendly antler contact.

LOUDNESS AND DURATION

All antler rattling sessions were 30 minutes in length and involved three 10-minute segments. But each session varied in loudness and duration. For example, short and loud sequences involved one minute of loud rattling, followed by nine minutes of silence. A long and loud sequence involved three minutes of loud rattling, followed by seven minutes of silence. Bouts of low volume rattling, to mimic sparring, followed a similar pattern.

In addition, before rattling began, the individual doing the rattling broke nearby branches, rubbed trees, and scraped the ground to simulate bucks fighting.

Of the four antler rattling sequences tested, those two involving loud rattling attracted the most bucks. In fact, 73 percent of buck responses were to a loud sequence. Duration of rattling (one versus three minutes) did not influence buck response to loud rattling. In other words, bucks were most responsive to rattling that mimic fighting, whereas they were less likely to investigate rattling that sounded like sparring.

During loud rattling sessions, bucks were most responsive during the first of three rattling segments. By comparison, bucks were more likely to respond to the second segment of low volume rattling.

Bucks not only responded more frequently to loud rattling, they were quicker to respond and seemed more aggressive when they approached. Because of the locally high buck density, the researchers speculate that bucks become accustomed to the frequent sound of sparring and therefore are less likely to investigate low volume rattling.

OTHER FACTORS

With few exceptions, rattling during the morning hours (until 10:30 a.m.) was most productive. However, long and loud rattling produced significantly better results during the afternoon hours (1:30-4:30 p.m.). But keep in mind, even midday rattling can be effective.

The researchers found no relationship between buck response to rattling and temperature. However, probably as expected, buck response rates were highest when winds were light and decreased as wind speeds increased.

Most (60 percent) bucks that responded to rattling were first sighted downwind. This seemed to suggest bucks used wind direction to determine the location and/or source of rattling, and even maneuvered from other positions to approach from downwind.

Based on observations of radio-collared animals, bucks apparently did not learn to avoid antler rattling. In 13 of 14 rattling instances, individual bucks responded to successive rattling sessions. One buck responded on all four occasions that a rattling session was performed nearby.

CONCLUSIONS

Many so-called deer antler rattling experts recommend going through a multitude of unnecessary gyrations, such as first "tickling" the antlers together gently, in order to attract a buck. The research discussed here indicates that's a bunch of bull — the whole process is really quite simple.

If you hope to attract a decent buck into killing range via antler rattling, the quickest and best way is to bang the damned bones together good and hard for about a minute during the rut.

On the other hand, since mature dominant bucks are probably tending does during peak-rut, the best time to attract a monster buck might be during early-rut, late-rut, or even post-rut.

If you can't lure a buck into view, within 20-30 minutes, following one minute of loud rattling, your chances of success probably will dwindle with time. Then, you're better off trying another spot. Surprisingly, even older bucks apparently do not learn to avoid rattling.

Certainly, this study is not the last word on how to rattle in a big buck —which the researchers acknowledge. Obviously, the chances of success decline with decreasing deer population density and poor sex-age structure, and will likely depend upon visibility as well as other unknown factors. But under the right conditions antler rattling can be very effective.

Will antler rattling work in your area — or mine? I don't really know. But after reading this report, I'm gonna give it a darn good try. ∎

chapter 16

HUNTING HIS HOME TURF DURING THE RUT

JEREMY FLINN

▶ TRYING TO COVER A SINGLE buck's massive range during hunting season is nearly impossible, but just like us, every buck calls a much smaller area "Home."

Any seasoned hunter could tell you about a tree stand or old, fallen oak he just knew was the perfect spot. It had everything a big buck could want: food, water and thick cover, all within a short distance. Trees were ripped apart from antlers crashing against them, and scrapes were the size of helicopter landing pads. If there was a place a big buck called home this was it.

Unfortunately, most of these stories do not end by pointing to the shoulder-mount on the wall. Often, not only was there no buck shot, but there also wasn't even a buck seen in the area! With everything a buck could want in a short distance, and all the heavy sign, how could it be missed?

The area a buck calls home during the hunting season is typically 8 to 10 times smaller than its entire home range, or about 100 to 150 acres. This territory is what we refer to as his core area and where he spends at least 50 percent of his time. Most people spend at least half of their time at their home, with the rest split between work, grocery store, picking up the kids at school, etc; together, it creates our home range. Just like us, a buck feels extremely comfortable in his home and knows every inch.

All this information generates the question that if a buck knows the area he calls home so well, like us in our own houses, do we really have an advantage hunting his core area or are we just increasing the risk of bumping him out of the area for good?

HOW HUNTABLE IS HE?

Once you have identified a buck's core area or home, the first step is to determine if the area is favorable to hunting. You're probably thinking if this is where he spends at least 50 percent of his time, why wouldn't it be huntable? For starters, if he is sticking in a 4-year-old clearcut or cutover the odds of you getting into a position to kill him without spooking him are not good. Even if you get into the jungle, are you able to have adequate shooting lanes? The more disturbances you make in the area, the more likely he will be long gone.

It is extremely likely you will encounter some form of this when attempting to hunt this core area. Common sense says if this is where a buck spends at least 50 percent of his time, it will include a secure bedding area. But the entire core area probably will not be one giant bedding area, giving you the opportunity to catch him moving to and from food sources.

The challenge comes when countering a deer's natural instincts to move at dawn and dusk, or what is called crepuscular movement. What typically happens is a mature buck uses his core area under the cover of night. Even though he is there, we can't hunt him! To avoid getting in his living room at the wrong time and pressuring him out, set up trail cameras along the edges of the identified core area and begin developing a pattern for your target buck(s). You will quickly begin to realize if it is huntable in the morning or afternoon, and if you have to wait until a certain time during the season to begin hunting his home.

BE VERY, VERY, QUIET...

The line made famous by cartoon character Elmer Fudd unbelievably has some truth to it! Think of it this way: once you get into his core area, you have essentially entered his house. Picture this ... you come home from work, kick off your shoes, grab a beverage from the refrigerator and plop down on the couch with TV remote in hand. It would not take very long to notice an unusual creature hanging from your ceiling fan, would it? It may not be as drastic with a buck since his living room is much bigger, but he'll notice if something is out of place. This is why we often install tree stands months in advance, so deer can get used to them.

We hear repeatedly that the fewer disturbances in his home, the more likely he is to stay put. That ranges from hunting the area to just passing through. But I'm sure you are thinking that obviously you are not going to have a chance to get him by not hunting there! You're right, but there is a difference between hunting smart and hunting a lot. Some of my best hunts have happened the very first time I sit a spot. Maybe it is just coincidental, but I think the minimal disturbance at that spot played a factor. By planning your hunts based on weather conditions and trail camera results, you can hunt the buck's core area effectively with less risk of bumping him.

SUCCESS LIES IN THE DETAILS

If you think you are going to march right into a buck's core area, climb in the stand, and put him down, then good luck! Although it will happen on rare instances, the majority of the time it takes intense attention to details and planning.

One of the most common actions that will ruin your chances at killing a buck in his core area is the way you arrive and depart. Hunters often will bump deer walking to their stand and believe it "wasn't that bad" since it was under the cover of darkness. Wrong! Any disturbances can instantly imprint on that buck and without any notice he could disappear. Typically, you can get away with one or two of these; however, when it occurs pull up an aerial map and identify a new route to get to your spot to avoids those areas.

Additionally, although not hunting a spot enough can cause you to miss an opportunity, over-hunting a spot can be even worse. If the buck you are after regularly moves through his core area during daylight hours, there is no need to hunt the same spot morning and afternoon five days in a row.

Use your knowledge of his movements through observations or trail cameras to set up additional stand locations in the vicinity. By moving 40-50 yards from your initial stand, you not only relieve disturbance but also create a new opportunity to hunt a secondary trail the buck uses. This could be the difference between success and failure, particularly when pursuing mature bucks with archery equipment.

BY INVITATION ONLY

Only when you have carefully planned out your attack should you hunt his core area. Preparation has been constant since last season from finding sheds in a known bedding area to capturing him on trail cameras throughout the summer. You placed your stands in the summer, long before hunting season to allow him to adapt. You know he is in there, so when is it time to hunt?

Whether you have 50 or 500 acres, one wrong move could waste all your hard work. I like to place trail cameras right next to my tree stands. When I am not in my stand, I want to know everything and anything that passes through. If the buck I am after is showing up only at night, why risk bumping him and hunt?

As you photograph the buck through the season, you begin to see changes from 2:30 a.m. to 3:15 a.m. to 5:55 a.m. The more he shows up, the more you learn about him. Once he is getting within 30-60 minutes of shooting light, study the upcoming weather conditions and move in. With all the stars aligned, you have given yourself the best opportunity to kill him on his home turf.

WHEN, WHERE IS MY BEST SHOT?

Although a buck may spend at least half of his time in his core area, that doesn't mean he will be the most vulnerable to hunting while in there. As discussed above, many times these core areas are focused around major bedding areas. Often this prevents us from getting too close, and has him on lockdown during daylight hours. Regardless, you still stand a great chance at killing him in his core area. But sometimes making a move on him outside this area can pay big dividends.

There are only a handful of times (if that) when a mature buck is vulnerable during the hunting season. Most of those fall during the rut when his brain takes a temporary leave. Often you will catch bucks chasing does in their core area, but a buck is never more vulnerable than when he is out of his element.

Research shows that many bucks take wild excursions away from their territory. These trips make the buck extremely vulnerable, as he is no longer in a place where is knows every inch of dirt, but rather in unfamiliar area and often love struck while trailing a doe. Moving distances of more than three miles in a just a couple days has made him much more active and, therefore, visible to hunters.

During the rut, many hunters encounter bucks they have never seen before, and it is likely a buck on an excursion. It doesn't have to be a three-mile trip to make him vulnerable. Once he leaves his core area he instantly becomes less familiar with his surroundings, which may give you a slight advantage. A mature buck out of his comfort zone can increase your odds, but it also increases the odds of surrounding hunters.

Killing a buck during one of his trips takes more luck than skill. You can identify the way he is coming to and from your property, but if your timing is off then your work goes to waste. Use this knowledge to your advantage and like a core area, think on a smaller scale.

In most areas during the hunting season, a mature buck's core area on average

will be 100 acres. However, depending on the properties surrounding you, the average core area may be only 50 acres; especially if you are bordering never-ending crop fields or residential subdivisions. A buck will likely make dozens of trips a week out of his core area into the remainder of his home range to feed, drink, or search for does. These "mini-trips" become your best chance to catch that buck in more unfamiliar ground, and anyone who has hunted long enough knows you need to take every advantage given to you!

These are also the times when bucks disappear from your property. Many times they were killed or hit by a vehicle far from your land, and unless it was a giant, you never hear about him. This is the kind of stuff that drives a serious deer hunter crazy! The "what ifs" begin to run through our heads, and when we truly don't know what happened to him bothers us most of the season.

Hunting mature bucks is often frustrating. The unpredictable movement, and sensitivity to hunting pressure, have highly educated these deer to avoid hunters. But by identifying a buck's core area you have won half the battle, literally. Knowing where he spends at least half his time levels the playing field, and allows you to take the step up to the most exciting stage of hunting a mature buck … the pursuit! ∎

chapter 17

HOW TO CATCH A CRUISING BUCK

STEVE BARTYLLA

▶ AT FIRST GLANCE, THE STAND location didn't appear special. It overlooked the tip of a peninsula of tall grass, and two creeks met nearby. Sure, it had deer sign, but less than many areas of the farm. However, when I started looking closer, it made sense.

About 50 yards to the east, a long, wooded ridge tapered down behind the stand. Does bedded on top, and the sharp sides funneled deer up and down the point. A narrow wooded flat snaked along the creek edge where my stand sat, making for easy north-to-south travel along that sheer-walled ridge. About 150 yards to the north-west, a similar ridge produced the same effect, dumping deer into the peninsula in front of me. And there were more than 100 acres of head-high CRP to the southwest, serving as chasing and bedding grounds.

Finally, the banks of the creeks were very sharp and deep, creating a challenging obstacle. To get between the CRP field and either ridge, deer travelled through the peninsula, using the crossing on the larger creek 40 yards in front of the stand. Traffic to and from the eastern ridge crossed 20 yards down the smaller creek, where I sat.

The more I added it up, I realized my first glance had been wrong. The area seemed to lack an obvious pinch point, but closer inspection revealed that wasn't true. It served as an intersection connecting three distinct doe bedding areas.

One early-November morning revealed just how effective that type of a setup can be. At first light, a group of five bucks chased an estrous doe through the peninsula and down the eastern side of the smaller creek. Like tossing chum into a school of piranhas, that sparked a feeding frenzy of buck activity.

Attracted by the sounds of a chase, bucks seemed to emerge from every direction. Further whipped into a fever pitch from the estrus odors saturating the area, no doe was safe from being chased. At least 14 bucks passed within bow range by 9 a.m., most several times. It was incredible.

Just as the action waned, I spotted another buck approaching. He was one of the oldest bucks I'd ever seen, but his headgear fell short of what I was after. It wasn't until he turned his head that I recognized him. Though he'd gone downhill hard, I had no doubt he was the mid-160s buck I'd wounded at that farm three seasons before.

Knowing I had to correct my mistake, I came to full draw and told myself to slow things down. My pin settled, and I sent the arrow crashing home. Just like that, an amazing Illinois rut hunt had come to a close.

GRASPING THE BASICS

Many folks struggle when hunting the rut. It can be an extremely chaotic time — or flat-out dead. The day I killed that buck, I'd exchanged texts with a friend who was hunting his Illinois lease. He said the woods were dead and that it was too hot for bucks to move — just as I was experiencing unbelievable action.

No matter your approach to hunting the rut, you will experience some off days. However, if you approach it correctly, you might think you're drowning in bucks more days than not.

What are bucks seeking during the rut? Almost everyone knows the answer. Sure, bucks will feed and drink during the rut, but they are primarily after does.

So why would your rut hunts focus anything other than does? It's really that simple.

If you break it down, you'll likely find that most bucks you've taken during the rut revolved around does. This past shotgun season, I filled my second Illinois buck tag by rattling in a great buck. That might seem to be related to dominance more than does, but I'll bet my last dollar that deer was hoping to collect the doe the phantom bucks were fighting about. Of course, that's a safer bet because I had a standing buck and bedded doe decoy out.

My 2011 Wisconsin buck was cruising for does when I arrowed him by a pond. I arrowed a 2010 buck during the rut as he followed a doe. I killed another that year at

a funnel between two doe bedding areas. As I think about rutting buck after rutting buck, every deer's downfall was somehow related to does.

HUNTING FOOD AND WATER

Just because food and water aren't No. 1 on a buck's priority list doesn't mean hunters should ignore them. We just need to adjust our strategies.

Consider the Illinois shotgun buck I rattled in. During the early season, I'd bow-hunted that area hard. A huge 9-pointer had been coming out in the back corners of a field, so that's where I sat. I came close repeatedly but didn't connect. Still, I noticed the surplus of does that fed where the small bean field opened up into a huge cornfield.

On my return trip during the rut, that's where I headed with my shotgun. Hunting with Sugar Creek Outfitters, I was the only person on the farm and knew I'd be safe using decoys there. I set a tending buck over a bedded doe, just out from where the hidden beans met the corn, so deer could see them from great distances. The scene of several bucks chasing does around the decoy pair and the sound of rattling antlers was just too much for the buck to resist — so much that I pulled him in from more than 800 yards away.

When hunting food during the rut, you still need to hunt where the does are. If I had set up in the corners where the big 9 was coming out earlier in season, I never would have killed that buck.

Water holes are slightly different. I've found that water sources near doe bedding areas are far superior than other water holes does frequent. They draw from two potential paths to success.

The first applies to any water hole frequented by does. Mature bucks realize that water holes are potential hook-up locations, so they tend to cruise past them while searching. Wind direction plays such a strong role in checking does, so a downwind-side setup typically works best. The added bonus is that bucks will actively check nearby doe bedding areas.

Remember, during the rut, bucks are wearing their winter coats, and their activity levels are at an annual high. Though food and water might not be their primary motivation, you can bet cruising bucks are as thirsty as a marathon runner well into a race.

Also, deer breed many times during a condensed period. Bucks expend a lot of energy and can work up a thirst. Setups near doe bedding areas can take advantage of that, too.

I cashed in on that a few years ago. I had set up where several points converged by a deep pool in an otherwise dry creek. Does bedded heavily on the apexes of the points above.

I didn't wait too long before I saw a triple-beamed monster pushing a doe down the point. The buck was worn out, panting heavily with his tongue hanging out.

Three quarters down the point, the doe tried skipping the cut and heading up another point. With thirst apparently ruling the moment, the buck flanked and gouged her harshly in the side, pushing her back toward the water. Just before he began drinking, my arrow was in flight. The huge buck's need to rehydrate had let me tag him. Water sources near doe bedding areas can be fantastic places to catch rutting bucks.

DOE BEDDING AREAS: WHERE IT'S AT

Doe bedding areas can't be overhyped. During daylight, the best way for mature bucks to find receptive does is to go from bedding area to bedding area. That's where most of the does are during that time.

The reason I keep referring to mature bucks rather than bucks in general is that mature bucks act differently than immature bucks. Youngsters don't know what they're doing, and it shows in their pursuit of does. Conversely, that big, mature buck knows exactly what he's doing and balances minimizing energy expenditures with maximizing the odds of finding his target.

You can see this when comparing how mature and immature bucks check doe bedding areas. The youngsters learn that doe bedding areas are where the action is, but they haven't yet determined how to best check them. They commonly go blowing in, randomly chasing any doe they find.

A mature buck has learned that one pass on the downwind side tells him everything he needs to know. That approach minimizes wasted efforts and maximizes results.

Therefore, doe bedding areas with defined edges offer great setups on the downwind side. Small thickets, wetlands and CRP fields that hold does and have defined edges can produce dynamite action. Stands on the downwind edge of thicket bedding areas have produced many of my rutting bucks.

There often isn't a defined trail for scent-checking bucks, leaving you wondering where to place your stand. I've learned that about 20 yards off the prevailing downwind edge is about right. That placement allows for shots at bucks cruising the edge and out to 40 yards. When paired with the best trail accessing the cover, that's a great setup.

Doe bedding areas are also good spots to pull out scents. Bucks are already fixated on scenting estrous does, so they're much more likely to fall for the lie being sold by a top-end estrous scent.

One productive strategy is to place two scent wicks about 30 yards apart near the edge of the bedding area. Orient them so an imaginary line between the stand and wicks create a triangle. That can be a big help in stopping and positioning a buck for a shot. It also helps attract bucks that are downwind of your setup, cutting them off before they can wind you.

Unfortunately, not all doe bedding areas allow for such setups. Many are generalized areas or high ground not suitable for scent checking. In either case, you can set up in the middle of the action. It's risky, but I've pulled that off on a couple of great bucks. However, you'd better beat the deer into the area, take odor control to the maximum and be prepared for an all-day sit. Even then, hunting such setups more than once or twice a season typically ruins them.

Another option is hunting the best access to these areas. In some situations, topography or well-defined travel patterns make this a very successful approach. Still, the best setups are funnels that separate two or more doe bedding areas. To find the ones that don't stick out, plot on a map where does typically bed, and determine the best routes between them. This will help reveal hidden funnels.

CONCLUSION

Hunting does during the rut isn't ground-breaking, but many of the best hunting methods aren't. Most hunters realize that but still fall into the trap of hunting stands that have nothing to do with does during the rut. After all, they've seen bucks at other areas. When the rut hits, throw that out the window. The bucks have. Their primary concern is does. Make it yours, too. ■

chapter 18

CALLING MATURE BUCKS

JOE LIEB

▶ ONE NOVEMBER DAY DURING THE mid-1980s, I went out for what I thought would be a typical afternoon bow-hunt. The weather was perfect, and I was fired up.

Since that day, I've perfected my calling techniques for big deer. These tactics won't work every time, but they will make you more successful.

AN INTRODUCTION TO VOCALIZATIONS

On that November day, I pulled into my spot about noon. The area featured a valley that was about 1½ miles long and 200 yards wide. The valley floor was covered with second-growth timber choked with weeds and multiflora rose bushes, with the exception of a 5-acre cornfield on the northern end. Three draws converged north of the cornfield, and deer used those as travel routes to the corn from their bedding areas on hillsides and hilltops. It was tricky getting there, but that's where I wanted to hunt.

After an uneventful 90 minutes on stand, I caught movement about 150 yards away on the hillside to the east. A 160-class 10-pointer was slowly and deliberately walking toward me.

He closed the gap to about 70 yards when I heard a grunt on the hillside to the west. I soon spotted a doe about 50 yards away. About 50 steps behind her was a 140-class 10-pointer. Just as I saw him, he started after the doe. Although I'd heard trailing grunts before, that marked the first time I'd seen the buck and doe when it occurred.

Because of the terrain, the 160-inch buck on the eastern hillside couldn't see the buck and doe across the valley. However, he was facing toward them at full attention. I looked back to the west and saw the doe had run south about 40 yards and stopped. The 140-inch buck closed the distance between them to about 20

yards, trail-grunting all the way. Then the doe let out five bleats.

The 140-class buck trail-grunted right up behind her. He immediately mounted her and let out some short, deep, fast-paced grunts — tending grunts. The doe took a few steps, and the buck slid off her back. Then he let out a long, loud, throaty grunt. He moved up, mounted the doe again and immediately started tending grunting. The doe started moving away again, and then I heard brush breaking from where the 160-class deer had been. I looked over to see him run across the valley floor to the breeding pair.

As the 160 approached, the doe ran a short distance and stopped, but the 140-class buck stayed put, staring at the doe and oblivious that the other buck was running right at him. The 160-class buck caught him in the left rear quarter and almost knocked him off his feet. The 160's antlers actually penetrated the smaller buck's hide with at least three points. The 140 regained his footing and ran over the hill with the other buck in pursuit. That was the last I saw of them.

I stayed in my stand until dark, but all I could think about was the scenario I'd witnessed. After the hunt, I spent a sleepless night in the back of my pickup, knowing a door had opened into the world of deer vocalizations — a world I hadn't realized even existed.

I wondered why the larger buck had reacted the way he did. Was it territorial, dominance, breeding or a combination? I also wondered if I could duplicate what I'd heard well enough to achieve the same response.

ACT 2

I practiced doe bleating by mouth and grunting with my grunt tube, an older non-adjustable type that sounded good but had the pitch of a second-year buck. After about a week of practicing, I was confident enough to take my new technique to the woods.

That first night out, I didn't get any response to my calling. However, I saw a 140-inch buck trailing a doe about 80 yards away, and I learned my first calling lesson: It's an exception to call a buck way from a doe he's trailing. And of course, the closer the doe is to being ready to breed, the more difficult that becomes.

That season closed without any great success, except for the knowledge I gained. The next year, I had a new Quaker Boy grunt tube with an adjustable reed. I couldn't get what I considered to be a great doe bleat out of the call, so I continued to do that by mouth. I could produce a deep, somewhat raspy mature buck grunt that sounded excellent. My reasoning for using a deeper buck grunt still rings true: I want to sound like the caliber of animal I'm trying to call in.

I realized my calling was breeding oriented, so I waited until the chase phase of the rut was in full swing. I set up on a saddle on a timbered hillside. In front of the saddle, to the east, the hill dropped about 75 yards to the valley floor, where there was a 10-acre cut cornfield.

It was a perfect morning: overcast and cold, with a slight northwesterly breeze. Just as it got light enough to see, two small bucks walked through the saddle scent-checking for does. About 20 minutes after they left, I started calling. Just as I finished my sequence, I saw a huge buck step out of the brush at the edge of the cornfield across the valley below. He stared toward me for a few minutes, and then started walking south along the edge of the field. He was moving with a purpose, like he had somewhere to be. I couldn't understand why he didn't cross the cornfield and come to the call. After he walked about 50 yards, I called to him again. He stopped and looked toward me briefly, but then looked straight ahead and started moving again. I lost sight of him as he rounded the corner of the hill to the south.

I immediately lost faith in my newly discovered calling technique. A thousand questions entered my mind, and I didn't have an answer for any.

Five minutes after I last saw the buck, I figured I had nothing to lose, so I called again — with no results. After a few minutes, I figured I'd try once more and then quit. As I got about halfway through my sequence, I glanced to the south toward the end of the saddle. The buck was 60 yards away, staring right at me. He had me made, and there was nothing I could do about it. We stared at each other for a couple of minutes, and then he turned around and slowly walked out of sight. I still remember my last look at that huge rack as it disappeared.

LESSONS LEARNED

It's good that I couldn't read that buck's mind during our stare down, because I would have felt worse. His thoughts probably started with "stupid."

When I climbed out of the stand that morning, I had replayed every minute of the hunt in my mind 1,000 times. Although I was disgusted with the outcome and my nerves were frazzled, I understood the mistakes I'd made. I was also on my way to learning a new aspect of bow-hunting that would give me more respect for the intelligence of a mature buck.

I believe the typical grunt most deer hunters use is more of a social call than we like to believe. It's a common sound, and because of that, you can only speculate about how a mature buck will respond to it. Yes, grunts call in countless whopper bucks each year, but think about some of your experiences with grunting. Have you ever had a big buck stop at your grunt only to look toward you for a minute before continuing on his original path? Me too. No amount of grunting would bring him back, would it? Exactly.

When you're after a true monster buck, you must talk to him in a way that threatens his territorial and dominant instincts. You're trying to make him believe there's another mature buck in his area breeding does, so you'll want to wait for the correct phase of the rut before using this strategy.

I start my calling sequence with a deep, guttural trailing grunt of a mature buck. These are fast paced and about 20 vocalizations. Then I utter four to seven doe bleats that are long and drawn out; each lasting about three to four seconds. I then let out about 10 to 12 trailing grunts, three to five doe bleats and then a tending grunt. That sequence lasts about 15 seconds, and each vocalization is short and very fast paced, with the last grunt in the sequence consisting of a full breath blown through the tube as loud as possible.

While blind-calling, I'll run through that sequence every 20 to 30 minutes. When I'm calling to a buck I can see, I run through the sequence just enough for him to start coming in. By then, he knows my exact location and has already committed to respond. Any more calling can give you up.

Also, be creative. Bring a sapling or bush into the stand, and slap it off the side of the tree while you're calling. Or put a decoy out where a buck that's responding to your call can see it. That's one of the deadliest setups I know.

Will this calling technique bring in mature bucks 100 percent of the time? Not a chance. However, I've had much more success at calling in mature bucks than I've had with rattling.

If you use calling as a tool, perfect it, and put it in your bag of tricks, you will be more successful. ■

chapter 19

MASTER THE RUT

CHARLES J. ALSHEIMER

▶ MORE THAN 50 YEARS OF studying whitetails has taught me that there is no short cut when it comes to hunting them, especially during the rut. True, there always will be hunters who win the whitetail lottery by stumbling into an opportunity of a lifetime.

But successful hunters know a process is involved if they expect to successfully harvest rutting bucks year after year.

What follows are 15 ways I've used over the years to harvest rutting bucks.

1. LOCATE FOOD & BEDDING AREAS

The two driving forces in a whitetail's life are food and sex. Everything about them revolves around these two things. So, if you want to be a master of hunting the rut you'll need a keen understanding of where a property's prime food and bedding sites are located. As basic as these two things are I'm always amazed by the number of hunters who have a difficult time figuring this out. In short, locating both will determine the kind of hunting you'll have when the rut rolls around, because he who has the best food and bedding will have the deer.

2. MAP THE WIND

Just because you know where the prime feeding and bedding areas are doesn't mean you'll be able to hunt these locations successfully, because of wind currents. Over twenty years of raising whitetails has taught me that once they identify an odor, be it man, beast, or food, they will never forget it. Consequently, determining how air moves around a hunting location is a critical piece to the rut hunting puzzle that must be solved. Because of this I encourage all hunters to map and record how wind moves on the property they hunt.

Air currents change seasonally so the wind mapping should be done during the rut time-frame. And, be sure to map the wind at the elevation you hunt at because air currents often flow differently from 20 feet high than they do on the ground. I map wind currents using liquid bubbles, the kind kids play with. When blown from a plastic wand (that comes with the bottle) the floating bubbles visibly show how the air flows. The bottom line is if the wind isn't right don't hunt the location because if you do you'll do one of two things: turn the deer nocturnal, or cause them to move to another location.

3. HUNT TRAVEL CORRIDORS

Locate a ribbon of cover that affords deer the path of least resistance or the most cover as they travel from one block of cover to another. Bottlenecks are typically saddles in hillsides, ridge lines, benches on hillsides, river crossing, diversion ditches, hedgerows, or any thin cover that deer use as a travel corridor between their bedding and feeding area. One way you will know if a particular bottleneck is being heavily used during the rut is by the number of rubs and scrapes you find in it.

4. MAKE MOCK SCRAPE LINES

One of the best ways I've found to enhance the amount of activity in a travel corridor is by making mock scrapes along the bottleneck's primary trail. I accomplish this by hanging two to five mock licking branches every 50 yards along the trail I'll be hunting over. Using plastic electrical draw ties, I attach a mock licking branch on an existing branch that hangs over the trail, about 5½ feet off the ground. If there is no existing branch over the trail, I attach the mock licking branch to a wire strung between two trees.

Once done, I expose the earth below each branch, which makes the site look like a natural, active scrape. I've used attractant lures on the branches, but have discovered they are not necessary because the mock scrapes will begin to be heavily used within 48 hours, with or without lures. Make sure whichever mock scrape you intend to hunt over has at least a 10-15 yard wide shooting lane to it because when a deer works the scrape it will often do so from the left or right side of the scrape. The last thing you want to happen is for the buck to work the scrape right in front of you but you can't shoot because branches are in the way.

5. SECURE YOUR SETUP

If the rut falls in bow season I like to find a tree along a bottleneck's trail that will not only carry my scent away from the trail but also give me the greatest amount of concealment. Unless the ground is uneven I seldom hang a bow stand higher than 18 to 20 feet, which is my comfort zone. I've found that if I have the air currents figured out this is more than high enough. A gun season rut setup should be in a bottleneck but in a location where you can see the most country to allow for longer shots, because you never know where the buck will show up. If possible, have your stand in place a couple months before the rut.

6. ENTER AND EXIT

In my mind this is one of the most important aspects of successful rut hunting. As a result I take great pains to ensure I can get in and out of my stand without deer noticing me. I do so by not walking on or over the trail I intend to hunt. I also will rake debris off the entry/exit path so I can get to my stand quietly.

7. TIME THE RUT

For those who have followed Wayne Laroche's and my lunar rut predictions, you know the rut varies a little each year. Unlike 2011, when the rut was cranking from Nov. 9-20, this year's rut will be earlier. This year the rutting moon (second full moon after the Autumnal Equinox) will shine full on Oct. 29, triggering the rut's onset.

Because of this hunting should be spectacular from Oct. 28 through Nov. 12, with the peak rutting activity in the North being Nov. 1-10. By Nov. 12 the breeding phase of the rut will be in full swing, causing deer activity to slow, when bucks are locked on estrous does.

8. CHANGE WITH THE RUT

I view the rut as having three phases: seeking, chasing and breeding. During the seeking and chasing phase bucks are on the move looking for does. This is when they are most vulnerable and easiest to kill. When the breeding phase kicks in hunting gets tough and requires a change in strategy. With nearly every buck locked on to a doe during the breeding phase a hunter's strategy should now turn to hunting doe groups, because this is where the action will be.

9. DON'T PRESSURE

In order to have daytime deer activity you have to convince deer there is no human presence in their core area. The only way this can be accomplished is by staying out of their bedding and feeding areas.

If you use trail cameras make sure they are placed in locations not commonly frequented by deer when you normally would check them. I accomplish this by positioning trail cameras along inside corners of well-used food plots and check them only every 3-4 days, and only in the middle of the day. To insure that all deer using the food plot are being photographed I hang mock licking branches 10-15 feet in front of the camera. This keeps my scent and the chance of me being detected to a minimum.

10. MORNINGS OR EVENINGS?

Two hours either side of darkness is the magic time to hunt during the rut. But don't overlook the 10 a.m. to 1 p.m. time frame because during the rut there is a spike in buck activity during mid-day. If you want to take a break in hunting I'd suggest doing it between 1-3 p.m. Over the many years Wayne Laroche and I have conducted our lunar rut study, our camera data has shown that 7:30 a.m. to 8:30 a.m. is the greatest period of daytime deer activity during the rut. The next highest period for deer activity is the last hour of daylight.

11. BE A WEATHER WATCHER

Whitetails seem to have a built-in mechanism to alert them of impending changes in weather, even if the sky is clear. When conditions are changing their feeding can increase dramatically prior to the arrival of bad weather and after a storm has passed. A number of studies have been completed regarding the effects of barometric pressure on whitetail activity. In one, Illinois biologist Keith Thomas found that the greatest whitetail feeding occurred when barometric pressure was between 29.80 and 30.29 inches. So, when the barometer is falling or rising through this range, deer activity should be greatest.

12. HUNT DOE GROUPS

A word to the wise: think seriously about hunting doe groups when Nov. 5 rolls

around. When breeding starts and goes full blown bucks will abandon their normal travel corridors and make fewer rubs and scrapes. This year, from Nov. 5 to 18 in the North expect every whitetail buck to be hanging with does.

13. CALL 'EM CLOSE

Bringing bucks within range, both with a grunt tube and rattling antlers has revolutionized the way I hunt and increased my success immensely. In the last 25 years I've discovered deer are more responsive to a call than anything else. Regardless of where I hunt in North America, I find that for every buck I rattle in, up to 20 will respond to grunting, bleating and wheezing.

14. BECOME A DUPE MASTER

Hunters have been using decoys to kill whitetails in North America for centuries. After using them for more than 20 years I can say this about decoys: they can either be incredibly exciting or a real disappointment. The trick to having them work lies in knowing how to use them.

15. LEARN HOW TO EXECUTE

Most hunters will agree that becoming a successful deer hunter boils down to months of methodical preparation which culminates in 30 seconds of sheer excitement. Simply put, it's the last half-minute before the moment of truth that determines victory or defeat in the woods. As a result, "chance favors the prepared hunter" should be every rut hunter's motto.

All the successful rut hunters I know are masters of not only the previous 14 points, but the minor details as well. Details like target practicing incessantly so that when the moment rolls around their shot is clean and true. The best leave no stone unturned, even to the point of practicing what they'll do if things like having their arrow fall off the bow's rest when they come to full draw, or how they'll overcome muscles locking up to the point they can't pull their bow back on a cold morning. It's all about being prepared.

Repetition insures execution, which leads to victory ... and venison. ■

SECTION 3: POST-RUT

chapter 20

HOW TO HUNT THE LOCKDOWN PHASE

CHARLES J. ALSHEIMER

▶ WHAT IS PEAK-RUT? DO YOU know when it takes place?

If you ask five hunters to describe peak-rut, you'll probably get five different answers.

For many Northern deer hunters, peak-rut occurs when the woods explode with deer activity in November. It's when new rubs and scrapes are popping up everywhere. It's that time when helter-skelter chasing seems to be taking place in nearly every woodlot. Though these behaviors are what whitetail hunters live for, they actually aren't that common during peak-rut.

From a biological standpoint, peak-rut is that period when the majority of does are bred. In a fine-tuned herd, peak rut spans about two weeks. Even under the best of conditions, a small percentage of does will breed before and after this two-week window, but typically more than 75 percent of the does will come into estrus and breed in a two-week window. Seasoned hunters refer to this time as "lock down time." They also know that it can be the toughest period of the rut to hunt.

LOCKDOWN BEHAVIOR

During the weeks leading up to peak-breeding, bucks are very active. Their hormone levels are off the charts and their attitude index is at the breaking point. Sleep comes hard and eating nearly ceases as they frantically cruise from doe group to doe group.

For bucks, the seeking and chasing phase of the rut is all about presence, and they leave no stone unturned in their quest to let every buck and doe in their home range know they are ready for duty. In the process, it's not uncommon for remote and farm country bucks to cover more than 3,000 acres in a 48-hour period in their quest to locate an estrus doe in the days leading up to the breeding phase.

This pre-breeding period is when most whitetail hunters love to hunt because the action can be non-stop. Though exciting, it can be short lived because after the breeding phase begins, buck activity can seemingly crash overnight.

In a poorly balanced herd, where does greatly outnumber bucks and where a small percentage of mature bucks make up the population, every available buck is locked onto an estrous doe during peak breeding. In such herds, buck sightings can disappear overnight because a doe's home range is very small and they are far less active than bucks.

In reasonably balanced deer herds (two or three adult does for every antlered buck) with a good representation of mature bucks (2½ or more years of age), competition can bring about some very interesting rutting behaviors.

Often when a mature buck is tending an estrous doe, subordinate bucks will attempt to "horn in" on the mature buck's right to breed the doe. This creates what is commonly known as a breeding party. When this takes place, a doe fears for her life and often winds up being chased several hundred yards by the sex-crazed bucks. I've seen this scenario played out many times while hunting and photographing and the level of action is as intense as it gets. The chase usually ends with the doe slithering under a blow down to protect herself from the bucks. Also, when a breeding party forms, it's not uncommon for a vicious fight to take place between the dominant buck and the next highest ranking buck in the breeding party.

One of the biggest difficulties of hunting the lock-down phase of the rut is that, unlike the seeking and chasing phase of the rut, you never know where you'll find the estrous doe and buck or a full-blown breeding party. In most cases, the locations you hunt during the seeking and chasing phase aren't that great because of the unpredictable nature of whitetails during the breeding phase. You are just as apt to find a buck tending a doe in the middle of a fallow field or hedgerow as in the heart of the woods during this time.

Unless chased by a party of bucks, an estrous doe moves very little. In the farm country of western New York where I live, our farm is part of a telemetry study that was set up to monitor deer movement. Interestingly, most of the collared does cover about 500 acres during most of the year. However, during fawning season and the breeding phase of the rut, their movement is next to nothing. It's been my experience, from years of photography and hunting, that if an estrus doe is not pressured by multiple bucks, she might not cover an area the size of a football field during her 24-hour estrous period. Other than rising to urinate and allow the buck to breed her, she remains bedded when in estrus.

The number of times a buck breeds a doe is dependent on the doe. Once I photographed a dominant buck breed a doe eight times throughout a day. During the whole episode, the two moved less than 100 yards. Add to this the fact that an estrous doe smells right for up to 24 hours before entering estrus and 12 to 24 hours after cycling out of estrus, which causes the buck to stay with her. This is why deer sightings are tough to come by during the lock-down phase of the rut.

BEST TIME TO HUNT

After a doe cycles out of estrus, the buck will abandon her and move on to find another doe to breed. For this reason, buck activity can occur at any hour of the day during the lock-down period. So, unlike the seeking and chasing phase of the rut, when peak activity is two hours either side of darkness, you are just as apt to see a buck wandering around in the middle of the day looking for does. For this reason, I hunt the lock-down phase a little differently than the seeking and chasing phase.

Regardless of which phase of the rut I'm hunting, my journal entries show that the first two hours after daybreak are the best. The three hours from 10 a.m. to 1 p.m. are also very good. As a side note, the two bucks I've killed in my career that scored more than 170 came at 10:30 a.m. and 1 p.m. Both were harvested during the lock-down time as they cruised in search of does.

The last hour of daylight is feeding time for whitetails, regardless of what time of year it is. For this reason, I make it a point to be on stand two to three hours before nightfall, especially during the lock-down phase. Does dictate movement during the lock-down phase and are driven to feed at the end of daylight hours, even if they are in estrus.

WHERE TO HUNT

Deciding where to hunt during the lock-down phase is dependent on a few things. Stands used during the seeking and chasing phase will work well if they are common doe travel corridors near a prime food source. If lock down falls during bow season, my favorite set up is in pinch points or bottlenecks between prime bedding and feeding areas. During firearms season, my preference is to be able to see a good distance in at least two directions should a long range opportunity present itself.

In all cases, the wind has to be in my favor while hunting, entering and exiting the stand. If the wind isn't right, especially during bow season, I will not hunt the location. During lock down, if there is deer movement, the doe will be the first deer to appear, so if you spook her, you'll never get a chance at the buck following her. Because of this, I'm a stickler when it comes to dealing with wind currents.

STRATEGIES

Knowing how and when to use a call can be a deal maker during this phase. Two calls that can bring a buck in "on a string" are the doe bleat and tending grunt. I'll often use the doe bleat three to four times just before and after I do a rattle sequence. I'll also use it when the action is slow and I haven't seen a deer in a while. Basically it sounds like "neeeaaah." Several manufacturers make a bleat can and all work the same way — by tipping the can upside down and returning it to its upright position. I recommend using the biggest bleat can you can buy to ensure an out-of-range buck can hear the call.

The tending grunt can be a lethal weapon if used properly. When a buck is with a hot doe and is either frustrated by her rejections or is interrupted by another buck, he'll often make a medium tone grunt that has a ticking cadence. So, if I'm hunting thick cover and a buck walks through, I'll use a tending grunt to lure him to my stand. This is a great call to use when bucks are cruising and the breeding phase is boiling over.

Most view rattling as a strategy primarily geared to the pre-breeding phase of the rut. Though true, don't overlook it as a great strategy for lock-down bucks as well. Because fighting often occurs when a breeding party takes place, mimicking two bucks aggressively fighting can be a great way to bring a buck to your stand during the breeding phase. This is particularly the case when a buck cruises through your area, out of the range of a grunt tube's sound. If no buck is in sight, I'll aggressively rattle for no more than 1½ to two minutes, followed by two to three doe bleats. If nothing happens, I'll wait about 45 minutes and try again. Should a buck cruise past out of range, I'll clash the antlers together long enough to get him headed toward me, before putting them away to prepare for the moment of truth.

And don't rule out using a decoy during the lock-down phase of the rut because it can result in spectacular action. A strategy I like to use is placing two decoys — a standing buck and a bedded doe — close to my stand and in an area that an approaching buck can see. Place the bedded doe decoy within 5 yards of the buck decoy. Also, the buck decoy's antler size can play an important role in the set up. My best action has come when the buck decoy has yearling-size antlers. This keeps yearling bucks from cowering and fleeing the scene and mature bucks will be quick to move in to show their dominance.

Of all the phases of the rut, the lock down is by far the toughest to hunt. But even so, it can be the best phase of all to hunt for the hunter who has the know-how and patience to hunt this period. ■

chapter 21

IS THE SECOND RUT REAL?

STEVE BARTYLLA

▶ THE PREMISE IS SIMPLE: BUCK-TO-DOE ratios are so woefully out of whack there's no way all the does can be bred during peak breeding. It's also understood that does not impregnated cycle back into estrus 23 to 30 days later. So if you wait the number of days in the does' cycle past peek breeding, you've nailed the timing for the second rut.

That apparently provides hunters with a basic grasp of math a tremendous advantage. After all, because at least some does were bred the first go-around, there should be about the same number of bucks chasing fewer does. Therefore, bucks must search harder to find does and fight off even more bucks to win the right to breed.

At first glance, that seems logical. In fact, it sounds like a Northern or Midwestern hunter's dream. If it were true, I'd forget the rut and take the seemingly much more intense second rut every time.

There's only one problem: It's a dream, not reality.

After hunting "the second rut" more times than I can remember, I've still not seen a horde of bucks dogging a mature doe in early December. Sure, I've seen that occur with doe fawns. However, those activities are spread out from mid-November through the end of December, and research reveals that fawn breeding even occurs in January.

All of that begs the question: Is the second rut reality or fantasy? It will take a greater mind than mine to answer what occurs and why with the Southern rut, but it's actually fairly easy to answer that question regarding the North and Midwest.

The foundation the second rut is tragically flawed in three ways. As with almost anything, a flawed foundation makes the structure unstable.

The first problem regards horridly skewed buck-to-doe ratios. Research has revealed that achieving anything higher than 1-to-3 is almost impossible in the wild, and even 1-to-2.5 is tough to hit.

Of course, we're talking pure bucks to does, regardless of age. Those numbers hold true if you toss out the fawns. However, even on the best managed grounds, they're exceeded when referring to a ratio of mature bucks to all does. Using that criterion, you can achieve the wildly skewed ratios folks often cite. However, you can't when comparing all males to all females, even when tossing out the fawns.

The next problem involves breeding does. A 1½-year-old buck is just as capable as Mr. Big. No, he doesn't have the rutting rituals down. He wastes a lot of energy on lost causes and is relatively clueless. Still, research reveals that young bucks do a good share of the breeding, even in populations with healthy age dynamics. Heck, even nubbin bucks can breed after they hit certain developmental thresholds.

Finally, not all does enter estrus at the same time. Even in far Northern ranges, where the breeding window is tighter, some does come into season early, most on time and some late. Those that hit on time are spread out across a week or more, with that on-time window stretching to almost a month in the Midwest.

When you factor in everything, pitifully few — if any — does are missed during their first estrus cycle. Sure, some come in a bit later than normal, but that's usually because of injury, social stress, nutritional stress or reasons other than having been missed during their first estrus cycle.

THE FAWN FACTOR

The true foundation of the second rut is built on doe fawns. Surprisingly, many doe fawns can breed before their first birthday.

According to *Deer & Deer Hunting's* John J. Ozoga, the key to doe fawns achieving estrus is tied to attaining the threshold of fat-to-lean body-mass ratio necessary to achieve puberty. Many factors dictate if or when that will occur, including nutrition, social stress, environmental stress, health of the mother and the date of birth.

So it's easy to understand that doe fawns breeding during their first year won't fall into a neat timing window. In fact, that can occur anywhere from the later stages of peak breeding all the way through January.

Anecdotal evidence is never as solid as thorough scientific research. Still, it can be revealing. Throughout my 37 years of hunting the Midwest and points North, I've yet to see a mature doe exhibit signs of estrus in December or January. However, I've seen doe fawns do so many times. Though a few die-hard hunters I know have seen mature does show signs of December or January estrus, they agree that the number of estrous doe fawns they've seen during that time far exceeds the rare sightings of mature estrous does.

Because doe fawns are primarily responsible for the second rut, it's impossible to accurately predict when it will occur. In reality, it's spread out across a two- to three-month period.

When a fawn or two enters estrus, there can be a brief yet intense flurry of rutting buck activity.

However, it will be short-lived. The buck population would risk suffering very high mortality rates if it wasn't.

Mature Midwestern and Northern bucks are often in tough shape come December. They commonly lose 20 to 30 percent of their body weight during the pre-rut and rut. Many are also nursing wounds from fighting.

Meanwhile, winter offers survivors their seasonal low point for food, in quality and quantity. And you must figure in cold and snow, which stress bucks even more.

These bucks cannot survive an extra month or two of extreme rutting behavior. They simply must focus more on survival than breeding.

That doesn't mean bucks will pass up late breeding opportunities. However, they seem to pick their shots when going out of their way to find them. The days of spending 20-plus hours on their hoofs, doing nothing but searching for estrous does, are done. Their survival depends on it being finished.

THE FARM BELT IS WHERE IT'S AT

More than 70 percent of Farm Belt fawns can enter estrus during their first year. This strip of latitude typically offers a surplus of nutrition, comparatively mild winters and sufficiently low deer numbers to keep social stress at a minimum. Those factors help fawns achieve puberty their first year.

The obvious result of 70 percent or more doe fawns entering estrus is a much longer breeding season. In fact, the steady trickle of fawns can stretch breeding out well into January.

Though pockets of anomalies exist, that percentage decreases as you head north. In fact, during particularly bad years, no doe fawns enter estrus. However, during good years, that number can range from 5 to 20 percent, even for Northern fawns.

THE FOOD FACTOR

With quality food sources dwindling, the few remaining prime food sources can really attract deer during winter. These spots can let you take advantage of a buck's shift to winter survival mode and desire to take advantage of breeding opportunities.

Most late-season hunters realize that a blast of nasty weather gives Mr. Big incentive to get to a food source early. Nasty weather requires an increase in calories to maintain body heat, and late afternoon is comparatively warmer than the colder late night and pre-dawn. Feeding during late afternoon lets Mr. Big conserve heat and energy by bedding during colder time periods.

Meanwhile, where do does and fawns concentrate during the last hour or two of shooting light? Most often, at a food source. That makes food sources the best spots to find breeding opportunities during that time of day.

Because they facilitate winter survival mode and provide breeding opportunities, prime food sources are fantastic locations for meeting Mr. Big.

DECEMBER DYNAMITE: HUNTING SCRAPES

Mature bucks might not search endlessly for estrous fawns and few late does, but they're savvy enough to take some carefully planned shots. They're experienced and understand how to stack the odds in their favor.

One of those ways is revisiting heavily used family group bedding areas. While making a cruise of the downwind sides of these spots, bucks commonly reopen the most heavily used scrapes in the area.

That makes these scrapes great locations to set up for morning-through-early-afternoon sits during December. When the wind is blowing from the bedding area to a hammered scrape, sitting in a stand downwind of that scrape can be a midday producer when few other areas are.

CONCLUSION

The traditional view of the second rut is far more fallacy than fact. You will not see hordes of does miss out on finding a mate during peak estrus only to cycle back 23 to 30 days later. It just doesn't happen.

However, some does will enter estrus later than others, and there are doe fawns to consider. Add that together and some breeding occurs after the peak breeding phase.

Luckily for hunters, mature bucks appear to key in on these opportunities far more than younger bucks. No, they won't spend December and January running wild, but they take advantage of some opportunities. Understanding that can be the first step toward getting a crack at these monster second-rut bucks. ■

chapter 22

HOW TO HUNT
THE SECOND RUT

DON HIGGINS

▶ A SEVERE LATE-DECEMBER SNOWSTORM WAS headed my way, and I probably wouldn't be in the woods for a couple of days.

The snow started to fall during early afternoon, and I decided to risk an evening hunt before the roads closed. Knowing the severity of the storm, I figured any local whitetail would probably seek shelter in the densest cover available. I headed to a nearby thicket that was almost impenetrable with dense understory trees and shrubs, many of which were covered with green honeysuckle vines. If I were a deer, that's where I would wait out a storm.

As I got out of my vehicle and readied my gear, I noticed the wind had increased considerably. I started to question my sanity for hunting. With near-blizzard conditions expected to worsen, I changed plans. I wasn't sure how long the weather would let me hunt, so I opted to slowly still-hunt through the thicket rather than sit in my stand. Besides, I expected deer to be bedded rather than on their feet. With the wind and blowing snow, I might slip up on an unsuspecting whitetail.

Soon after entering the thicket, I saw lots of fresh deer tracks in the new snow. It was obvious my hunch was correct, and many deer were in the thicket. I slowly slipped along, thinking I would get a shot at a bedded whitetail at any minute. That never happened.

Instead of being bedded, the deer were milling about in the thicket, browsing on the green honeysuckle as they prepared to hunker down. I encountered several deer during that brief hunt, but instead of running from the cover to escape me, they simply trotted away and were swallowed up by the thick cover and falling snow.

A couple of things were evident. The thicket was loaded with whitetails, and if I didn't return to my vehicle and head for home, I might end up walking instead of driving. I vowed to return when the storm passed.

I was stuck at home the next day, knowing the whereabouts of numerous white-

tails. However, I could only look out the windows at the blowing snow that had shut down schools, businesses and even well-traveled roads. The next day, I awoke to sunshine and a light breeze. I knew snowplows would soon open the roads, and when that happened, I'd head for the thicket. As I ate lunch, I heard the welcome sound of plows and was soon off to spend the rest of the day at the thicket.

Having had almost two days to consider my options and plan the hunt, I decided to take my rattling antlers to the stand. I figured there were a few bucks in the thicket, and with so many deer in such tight quarters, I might dupe an older buck into believing the competition was squaring off over dominance or a hot doe.

I reached my tree stand without spooking any deer, but I discovered I had forgotten my tree steps. I always take out the bottom few steps to make it tougher for thieves to steal my stands. I had a decision to make: Should I walk back for the steps or find an alternative?

The back side of the front brought single-digit temperatures that were expected to fall below zero that night. The temperature would decrease as afternoon wore on, and I knew I would be hard-pressed to sit until dark. I also knew that if I walked back to get the steps and returned my stand, I would work up a sweat, and my sit would be brief — and colder. Also, I hadn't seen any tracks on the way to my stand and was starting to doubt if the deer were still there. I opted to find a hiding spot on the ground and rattle a bit. If nothing showed, I would leave in about an hour and warm up in my vehicle as I drove to another location.

I was soon in a downed treetop about 10 yards from the tree with my stand. I banged the antlers together, never believing a deer would show. But almost immediately, I had a 150-class 5-by-5 at 20 yards. The thick cover left little room for shooting lanes, but I found a small hole that gave my arrow an unobstructed path to the buck's vitals. However, my arrow hit a twig and sent the buck crashing away.

I waited a few seconds and hit the antlers again. Amazingly, the buck returned almost instantly and offered another tough shot through thick cover. I found another hole, but the buck caught me drawing my bow and bolted again.

I grabbed the antlers and couldn't believe it when I saw the buck approaching again. This time, however, he was more cautious. At a distance, he worked downwind until he hit my scent stream and bounded away for good.

I sat dumfounded at what had just occurred. Then I heard a twig snap, turned my head and was eye to eye with a 140-class 4-by-4 looking at me 10 yards away. There was no chance with that buck, though. When our eyes met, he whirled around and left.

THE SECOND RUT?

More than 25 years later, that hunt remains one of my most memorable and also most frustrating. If only I had remembered those tree steps. It's also one of the few times I've witnessed rut-type behavior after the November rut. When I told another hunter about my rattling success that evening, he said, "The second rut must be happening."

That's probably similar to what many other hunters would say or think.

Outdoor writers have more power than we sometimes realize. We can turn unproven theories or even fabrications into accepted truths. Readers give credibility to the written word and accept it as truth, especially when it appears in respected publications. However, that's not always true. Articles can be somewhat biased or even false. That goes beyond hunting publications and includes respected newspapers and other news-reporting institutions.

I respect the credit I'm given by readers. I don't write anything I don't believe, and I don't use false stories or examples to promote an idea. I think some well-publicized ideas have been misrepresented or are better understood now than when they were originally promoted.

One of the greatest myths involves the idea of a second rut. Conventional wisdom holds that about 30 days after the peak of the November rut, there will be another flurry of breeding activity, or a second rut. Some writers and so-called experts have taken this further to promote a third rut, which would supposedly occur 30 days after the second rut. Each successive rut is said to be less intense than the previous one.

Hogwash. There's only one rut, albeit one that's often misunderstood because of false information. Let me explain why I believe there's only one rut and how it plays out.

THE ONE AND ONLY

In much of the whitetail's range, peak breeding period occurs in mid-November. During the middle two weeks of November, many mature does are bred, and smaller percentages are bred in the weeks before and after this period. In most herds, most does are bred during their first estrus cycle.

A commonly promoted second-rut theory is that some does aren't bred during their initial estrus cycle and cycle again 30 days later. I'm not saying this never happens, but I believe it's rare. Any buck can breed does, including most buck fawns. When a doe is in heat, it will stand for any buck to breed her. It doesn't care if the buck carries a world-record rack or is a button buck. In fact, a doe will let multiple bucks breed her when the time is right.

An experience from my farm convinced me a buck can smell an estrous doe more than a mile away. I have a small herd of captive whitetails I raise for study purposes. Each fall, I artificially breed the does. To do so, I give them shots to bring them into estrus. A few years ago, I was in a shed preparing for the breeding when I saw a wild buck approaching the pen containing the hot does. The buck walked across more than a mile of open farm fields toward the pen, with the wind in his nose. He was at the edge of our yard and was going to walk across — in daylight — to reach the does.

Because any buck can breed a doe and can smell them from long distances, almost every doe in most herds gets bred during its first heat cycle. Thus, the idea that a bunch of unbred does are waiting to trigger another miniature rut 30 days after the main event is false.

Sure, there's some breeding activity after the November rut, but that mostly involves doe fawns entering their first heat cycle. Promoters of the second-rut theory often mention doe fawns entering their first estrus cycles as being an additional trigger for the second rut. However, doe fawns don't come into heat at a specific time. A doe fawn is just as likely to come into her first heat cycle Dec. 1 as Feb. 1 — or any day in between. In fact, my experiences from more than a decade of raising captive whitetails and 30 years of hunting wild deer make me believe more doe fawns are bred during January than any other month in my area.

Again, this is just opinion based on my experiences, not a scientifically proven fact. Still, I believe most late-season breeding activity involves doe fawns and is random rather than occurring at 30-day intervals.

When I try to explain something to a beginner deer hunter, I often put the lesson in human terms to help them understand my point. This analogy might help you better understand the rut.

Think of the rut like the summer heat. The hottest days typically occur in August, just as peak whitetail breeding happens every year in November. As summer turns to fall, there's still some hot weather in September and even October, just as there will be some whitetail breeding in December and January. Those later hot spells are as unpredictable as late whitetail breeding activity.

You cannot mark on the calendar every year that there will be a miniature summer Sept. 15, nor can you say there will be a second rut every Dec. 15. When a September hot spell hits, we don't say, "Yep, there's that second summer." There's only one summer and one whitetail rut.

PLANNING FOR SUCCESS

Understanding how the rut plays out helps you plan. When you're fortunate to encounter a hot doe late in the year, the action can be terrific, because the doe might have every buck in the woods on her tail. However, the action will be short-lived, as she will only be in estrus briefly. I've seldom been able to take advantage of late-season rutting activity. In fact, I've only killed one buck because of late-season breeding behavior. That happened a couple of years ago, when a doe fawn in estrus led a mid-150-class 4-by-4 past me one January evening.

When I recall the experience detailed at the beginning of this article, I guess that a doe fawn might have come into estrus while the deer were holed up in that thicket during the snowstorm. When I rattled the antlers, they were ready for action. I was too — except for the tree steps I left in the vehicle. ∎

chapter 23

COSTLY MISTAKES:
7 WAYS TO MESS UP A
LATE-SEASON BOWHUNT

DANIEL E. SCHMIDT

▶ BOWHUNTING LATE-SEASON WHITETAILS IS OFTEN a lesson in humility. Big bucks all but vanish, and does, fawns and young bucks seemingly know which trails will lead them exactly 10 yards beyond shooting range.

Such is the life of a diehard late-season bowhunter. When you start taking things for granted, Mother Nature quickly deals you a sobering hand.

I've lived in the North my entire life and have hunted deer across the region. Although I believe farmland deer are much easier to hunt than their Northern Forest cousins, hunting them requires basically the same approach. Unfortunately, it has taken me weeks, months — and sometimes several seasons — of late-season bowhunting to truly unravel how deer use a piece of private or public land after mast crops all but disappear.

Whenever people ask me how they should approach late-season bowhunts, I counter by telling them what they shouldn't do — based on all of the mistakes I have made through the years.

Here is a brief list of seven deadly late-season bowhunting sins.

1. BANKING ON EARLY-SEASON STANDS

It is amazing how much changes in the deer woods in the weeks from opening day to the waning rut. Does acquire their grayish-blue coats, fawns pack on the weight and bucks become chiseled and blocky. There are good reasons for all of those things, and a lot of it has to do with the acorns, soybeans, corn, alfalfa and new-growth browse deer were eating not that far from the stands you hung for the mosquito-filled evenings of early fall.

It is awfully easy to leave those stands in place and run to them on weekends and the few spare hours you might find on a rare afternoon off in the late season. Huge mistake. No matter what size parcel you are hunting, late-season deer routes are often much different than those of the early season.

Take the time to find travel corridors deer use during the fringe hours of daylight. Brushy fence lines, overgrown pastures and bottlenecks in tamarack swamps are good places to start looking for stand locations. Cover is the key, especially after gun season. Deer move during daylight, but most of that movement will be in areas where they feel safe.

2. LETTING YOUR GUARD DOWN

Late season means cold weather, especially in the North. It's tempting not to shower before hunting when temperatures drop into the 20s and lower. Scent control, however, is even more important now than it is during the early season, because deer have been pressured for weeks.

Use scent-killing soap and shampoo, and thoroughly dry off — especially your hair — before heading out for the hunt. Even a hint of moisture will carry some human scent. Place your hunting clothes in a scent-free bag or plastic box, and don't dress until you're at your hunting area. I'll admit this approach isn't always feasible. In those events, I take a bed sheet that I've washed in scent-free soap and drape it over the seat of my car. I will not, however, put on my boots until I'm ready to walk to the woods. I keep them in a Rubbermaid container in the trunk of my car.

Before heading out, I spray my boots and pants cuffs with liberal amounts of scent-killing spray. I also brush my teeth with a baking-soda based toothpaste and pack an apple for a snack, which helps mask breath odor.

3. ALERTING WITH ALUMINUM

My favorite quick ladders, hang-ons and ladder stands are made of welded aluminum, but I seldom use them when hunting in late November and December. Aluminum stands invariably pop, squeak and make other deer-spooking noises when I shift my burly frame during cold-weather hunts. That's why I opt for steel. Many manufacturers offer quality steel steps, ladders and stands. The best ones secure to the tree with a chain, and they are whisper quiet when cinched tight.

This isn't to say all aluminum is bad. In fact, stands made from one-piece cast aluminum designs are deathly quiet. So too are stands made of carbon and other composite materials.

4. TRYING TO THINK LIKE A DEER

It doesn't work. Not for me, anyway. Deer are North America's greatest game animal because they're so unpredictable. We kid ourselves when we walk into the woods and place stands based on areas that merely "look good."

For consistent late-season success, you need to know where the bedding areas are and what foods deer are keying on. Don't worry if deer aren't bedding on the property you are hunting. Your property might be a travel corridor from the neighbor's pine plantation to the nearby farmer's picked cornfield. You'll put yourself in position for a shot by knowing the exact trails they use to get from Point A to Point B.

5. HUNTING FIELD EDGES

Field edges are great for seeing deer up close in September, but they're often terrible for hunting in the late season.

If you are after big bucks, forget about field edges altogether unless you have secluded fields. Field-edge hunting in the late season is usually an afternoon affair, and adult bucks usually enter fields at the cusp of darkness. If you simply want to fill a tag, place your stand inside the woods' edge in some cover. Such patches are often called staging areas, places where deer congregate before entering a field.

I've used this tactic to kill several deer. Adult does are among the wisest deer in the woods, and they often stand in these small patches of cover to survey a field before entering it. After deciding the coast is clear, they typically trot out of the cover and into the field without hesitating. Field-edge stands are usually unproductive for that reason — deer seldom pause long enough to give you a shot opportunity.

6. NOT DRESSING FOR SUCCESS

Staying warm and shooting a bow accurately do not go hand in hand. The bulky clothing you wore for gun season might be prohibitive to making a shot while twisting around the base of a tree. Jacket collars, cuffs and bulky sleeves can easily get in the way of the bowstring.

The best approach is to invest in high-tech underwear. This stuff is lightweight

yet keeps you warm on the coldest days. Outer layers should include pants and jacket that are insulated yet streamlined. A knit hat and quality pair of pac boots will also keep you warm where you need it most.

I seldom give plugs to specific companies, but it is wise to check out the Heater Body Suit from T.S.S. Equipment of Cleveland, Wis. The suit is almost like a custom-built sleeping bag. It has saved many of my late-season bowhunts because it allows me to dress very lightly. The suit includes a zipper that opens easily when it is time to stand and shoot.

Air-activated hand-warmers are also effective. I use them in my boots, pockets and hand-warming muff. When temperatures drop really low, I wear a kidney belt that accommodates three hand-warmers. Never place hand-warmers near your skin, and don't use them if you have poor circulation.

Whichever outfit you wear, be sure to dress in your late-season outfit and practice shooting from a treestand. Achieving consistent groups while wearing winter clothing is a lot more difficult than you might think.

7. GIVING UP EARLY

The virtues of patience and persistence are important for any type of deer hunting success, but for late-season success, you need to tattoo them on your psyche. Hunters who leave their stands early are the ones who usually go home with unfilled tags. To taste success, you need to stay to the bitter end on every hunt.

What many hunters don't realize is the deer they spook today will be a deer they probably won't see tomorrow. Therefore, you need to always be thinking of the future. For example, if a deer shows up after legal shooting hours, stay in your stand, and wait until it leaves or at least moves far enough away so you don't spook it leaving your stand. Busting a deer when you are on the ground isn't nearly as bad as having one see you in your stand.

CONCLUSION

One of the most exciting times to bowhunt whitetails is when fall gives way to winter and the throngs of gun-hunters have left the woods. It can also be one of the most frustrating.

Success can be had, however, by the hunter who spends extra hours afield studying deer behavior and adjusting his tactics accordingly. ∎

chapter 24

THE HEART OF THE MATTER:
HOW TO HUNT CORE AREAS

PATRICK MEITIN

▶ I THOUGHT I HAD WHITETAILS pretty well figured out by the time I moved to northern Idaho. I had killed some respectable deer — including a handful of bucks surpassing 155 inches — from a variety of habitats. So when I discovered my new backyard swarming with deer and began to pick up trophy sheds, I believed record-book success was all but assured. I tossed up some stands and awaited the September archery season opener.

Many of the sites involved only a five-minute walk out my door, so I enjoyed more stand time that first season than the five previous combined. That had pretty much been the point of the long-overdue move; less travel, more bow-hunting.

I passed some decent bucks during archery-only season, convinced the rut — during general season — would open the flood gates to giant deer. I finally had my own land and only a solid "archery-book" buck seemed appropriate to christen a new beginning.

The plan seemed to be coming together perfectly when the really big deer began to appear on camera in late October. However, by late November an acute case of disillusionment had set in. I had plenty of trophy-buck photos taking up space on my computer. Yet, not one was taken during daylight hours.

It became obvious my rural "neighborhood," with it's checkerboard of relatively small properties and gun-happy mentality had caused the biggest bucks to become understandably wary. The general season's opening weekend and the whole week surrounding Thanksgiving could be best described as all-out war. Only a nocturnal existence kept the deer alive.

I'd always understood this reality, but I was now being hit square between the eyes with it. Most hunters understand this dilemma — at least those living outside those golden Midwest lands where zero hunting pressure and skewed buck-to-doe ratios make the rules of engagement oh-so simple.

PATTERNING THE REAL WORLD

Patterning whitetails in an ideal setting is a simple matter of placing yourself between Point A and Point B at a creek crossing, woodlot funnel, cornfield edge or saddle where traveling bucks pass while making their rounds or ambling between feeding and bedding areas.

Patterning whitetails in the real world is different. The heavily-hunted woods of my backyard, Minnesota or New York, and the jungle-like terrain of the Deep South are examples of the tough, real world assignments I've faced while bow-hunting whitetails. Bow-hunting in these areas usually means discovering that one magical place where a trophy buck might actually arrive during legal shooting hours. This typically revolves around bedding areas. More specifically, it means finding core-use areas — those few acres where a buck spends the greatest majority of its time.

Simply, a core area is a piece of real estate where a deer is disturbed least often and feels most secure. While core areas might seem pretty obvious on paper, finding them can be confusing in practice. For one thing, a core area and the hours a buck keeps, can change with the season.

Early season deer, for instance, are still living off a fat summer with little hunter activity. They might freely venture into broad daylight in areas where food is plentiful. This can also happen during late seasons, when rut-worn bucks venture out seeking survival food thanks to slackening hunting pressure.

Early and late season core areas are subjects for another time, however. This article is about discovering a buck's most secret retreats and daytime movement patterns during the heart of hunting season.

FOLLOWING THE CAMERA TRAIL

For better or worse, trail cameras have changed whitetail hunting forever. They are unobtrusive, on the job 24/7 and present information in a straightforward manner — no deciphering spoor or reading into what sign is actually telling you.

A buck shows up on camera or he doesn't. It's that simple. And when he does, you gain insight into his world; the hour, temperature, where he's headed. If you catch him regularly, you own a little piece of his life.

The problem with trail cameras is they often prove downright frustrating. Thanks to mature bucks' nocturnal tendencies, dispirited trail camera users often ask if it would just be better to not know the buck is even there. I used to ask myself that question all the time — until I became more proactive in camera deployment.

Nowadays, I keep six or eight cameras working at any given time — and I need more — because when a mature buck begins to show up at a particular site, I begin a game of camera tag. Like a chess match, I begin pushing cameras away from the site in an attempt to discover the buck's origin: his core-use area.

Sometimes my camera tag ends in more frustration. But I've also managed to capture bucks up to a half mile from a starting point.

This little game is part intuition, part woods skills. The starting location is usually an obvious focus point such as a natural funnel, fence corner, food plot, feeder or agricultural field. But as bucks move away from these finite locations their movements often turn random and sometimes counter intuitive.

Preconceived notions of the ideal travel-way can work against you. For instance, a buck might cut through a cedar swamp or across a tangled, second-growth alder ridge instead of traveling an obvious defunct logging skid or ridge crest. There might be no "trail," per se, to hang your camera near.

Therefore, I always at least attempt some amount of tracking in my quest to follow a buck away from a particular point. I might find nothing more than a few heavy hoof prints in soft soil, a visible wake in deep leaves, or a fresh scrape beyond my last waypoint, but it gives me clues on the buck's basic trajectory and gives me an idea where to try a camera next.

Like trailing a wounded animal, you'll invariably encounter snags and confusing twists along the way. But the smallest step forward sometimes reveals the next piece of the puzzle. Be patient. Take baby steps when necessary. This process can take weeks.

LET IT SNOW!

I've written about "snow days" often enough I'm beginning to fear redundancy. Yet there's no better way to gain insight into deer movement and pattern a single buck than to see where he has actually walked. Tracking deer in leaf and pine-needle clutter is well beyond most hunters' abilities, but the lightest skim of snow lays everything bare. I often learn more from a single morning of snow tracking than I could glean from an entire month of bare-ground scouting.

Tracking a single buck away from a camera that has recently captured him is to tread a fine line between insight and potential disturbance. A buck might tolerate being jumped from his bed once — maybe. But doing so on a regular basis is sure to alter his habits.

Old-fashioned horse sense normally tells me when to back off — often when I'm approaching an obvious bedding area such as a cedar thicket or sun-soaked alder ridge on cold days.

Close observation while scouting can reveal the general habitat the deer in your area prefer when bedding; be it weedy swales in CRP fields, ridge points in hilly terrain or briar thickets in wetter locations. It's often safer to set a camera near an exit route and let it tell you what you need to know than barge in and risk bumping the deer.

The obvious exception is days immediately following the season's close, when deer are still in survival mode and late-winter snows clearly reveal their movements and bedding sites. With the season over, pushing a buck out of his bed involves no dire consequences. He'll have ten or more months to get over it.

In fact, post-season scouting is often more productive than pre-season searches. If nothing else, it reveals general travel and bedding tendencies in your area. And it can sometimes reveal the core areas of bucks that have made it through hunting season.

LOGICAL CONCLUSIONS

Finding core areas is one thing. Assembling the information you've gained into a logical plan of attack can be more intimidating.

Hunting core areas is a study in timing and keeping disturbances to a bare minimum. It's extremely important to enter and exit stands during hours when you're least likely to bump your buck. In addition, it's imperative to create foolproof entry and exit strategies.

Hunting core areas of nocturnal bucks can be quite demanding. You must arrive and settle into your stand or blind well before the deer arrives. In the morning, that means getting on stand during the black-dark, wee hours. And while dark hours are the great equalizer, it does you little good if you have to cross your target animal's expected trail or bump a bevy of snorting does on the way in.

Evenings can be a prudent-man's approach. However, they require literally stalking into your stand adjacent to a known bedding area hours before sundown, then settling in for the long wait before darkness. Exiting your stand can mean waiting well after dark before making your way out of the woods.

Placing your stands to take advantage of topography that disguises your coming and going is the best tactic.

Deep ditches or creek beds make the perfect example, even if you are forced to don waders to remain dry.

When you are planning your approach the most important factor is minimizing scent, but it is also wise to make it difficult for deer to hear or see you. If this requires a convoluted approach, a longer walk and earlier wake-up, so be it. Remember, too, a red-lens headlamp keeps you safe in the dark but also less conspicuous.

Of course, actually placing your stand has the potential to unravel the entire program. Like approaching a roosted turkey in the early morning, attempting to get a jump on a buck often means pushing that fine line between getting too close (and alerting your target) and not getting close enough (deer pass only after shooting hours).

Don't dismiss the option of setting your stand late at night, when you know absolutely — thanks to your trail camera work — your buck is at a distant feeding location. Of course, the tree should have been quietly scouted and chosen well beforehand to make this exercise go more quickly.

OUTSIDE THE BOX

Radical conditions sometimes call for nontraditional approaches. It's easy to fall into a rut in whitetail hunting; sitting the same stands week after week.

But when hunting pressure pushes deer movement ever deeper into dark hours, success ultimately comes down to discovering a buck's core area, where that deer spends most of its time and where he's most likely to begin movement when you might actually see to shoot.

Sure, installing yourself in a morning stand by 3 a.m. and hanging stands well after the late-night news isn't part of the standard program. It simply isn't much fun. But nocturnal bucks can require these radical tactics.

The good news is these hunts are typically short in duration. I regularly slip back into bed after sitting only a couple hours past daybreak. By then, my target buck is either safely past or has already made a fatal mistake. ■

chapter 25

BEDDING AREA DEATH TRAPS

JOHN EBERHART

▶ EVER BEEN PERCHED ALONG THE outside edge of a bedding area during the rut only to hear the telltale sounds of bucks chasing does within the bedroom? If you've been hunting very long, you certainly have.

In the movies, you often see secret agents wait at the home of someone they want to take out. After all, homes offer people secure places to socialize and sleep. A similar ambush plan would surely work for taking mature bucks in bedding areas during the breeding season.

Does typically bed in known bedding areas, and during the rut, bucks search for and breed does. Therefore, bucks search bedding areas within their core areas — sometimes outside — for estrous does. When bucks find does, most daytime breeding occurs well within the secure cover of bedding areas. If you don't believe that, count the times you have witnessed a mature buck breed a doe in an area with minimal, if any, security cover. I bet it isn't many.

While hunting within bedding areas, I've taken two bucks that were breeding does, killed three bucks at active primary scrape areas and rattled in three bucks, of which I shot two. Bedding areas have many perimeter runways that traverse into a network of interior trails. Typically, they also have small openings that act as hubs of activity. I'm a percentage hunter who chooses locations offering the best odds for the time of day and season, and the odds of intercepting a buck along one of several perimeter runways are far lower than my chances while hunting within the core of a bedding area where the runways intermingle. The closer to the core of any destination location, the better. And a bedding area is a destination during the rut.

So why do so many hunters treat interiors of bedding areas as sacred sanctuaries? The answer should depend completely on the nature of their hunting area. Having bowhunted in several low-hunter-density states and many differing hunting-density areas in Michigan, I know the type of hunting pressure, or lack thereof, has more to do with how, when and where mature bucks move during daylight than any other factor. So the nature of your hunting area should be based on the type and quantity of hunting pressure it receives.

PROPER PERSPECTIVE

Hunting areas differ tremendously. To confirm that, just watch a hunting TV show or video. When you own or lease enough land— or hunt where somebody else does — where a buck can leave a bedding area and you don't have to worry about him getting killed by a neighbor, you can feel comfortable leaving bedding areas as sanctuaries where hunting is prohibited.

TV stars, video personalities and high-end property hunters prove year after year they can be successful outside bedding areas. They have the luxury of little or no hunter competition or hunt areas with strict kill criteria. These properties have many mature bucks that will roam outside security cover during daylight because of a lack of danger from previous hunter encounters as they grew to maturity.

When bucks sporting their first, second and sometimes third set of antlers have knowingly passed by hunters with no negative consequences, they have no reason to dramatically alter their daytime movement habits and become primarily nocturnal beyond the security of bedding areas.

The types of spots I'll discuss when suggesting hunting within bedding areas are properties that receive heavy consequential hunting pressure. These hunting parcels are small, hunter densities are high and most hunters target any legal antlered buck. In such areas, forget the, "I-leave-my-bedding-area-as-a-sanctuary-area" statement. In these spots, not strategically taking advantage of secure bedding area hotspots is a mistake.

Deer behavior from area to area can be staggeringly different. In areas with heavy consequential hunting pressure, no matter the season, mature bucks typically bed down within a secure area well before first light unless they're with a non-compliant hot doe.

Even if a mature buck doesn't typically bed at a specific area, if several does do, the odds of him passing through during shooting hours to scent-check them or being locked down with one are much greater than the chances of him passing down a perimeter runway, walking into an exposed short crop field or moving through open timber. No matter the amount of sign-posting or sign in general, it means nothing if it wasn't left or revisited during daylight.

Because enclosure studies are done in captive, non-hunting environments on herds with balanced age and sex structures, I typically consider them relatively meaningless for hunting in heavily hunted areas, where none of that criteria exists. Doe estrus cycles, however, whether captive or wild, are standard in the species, and studies show the breeding lockdown time with a doe can take up to 36 hours. During peak rut, most does will enter their breeding cycles, and the few mature bucks around will spend most of their time within secure areas in search of or breeding them.

Several times, I have seen a mature buck encircling a doe to force her back into security cover when his chasing pushed her into more vulnerable open areas. I've also taken two mature deer doing that. The point is that the normal movement patterns of does and bucks come to a screeching halt during the peak rut.

The hunting media leads us to believe that frenzied daytime chasing by mature bucks in open areas is the norm during the rut, but that just doesn't materialize. Let me emphasize that open-area chasing likely happens in areas many celebrities hunt, but it's definitely out of the norm in areas with heavy consequential hunting pressure, where there are few mature bucks to compete for breeding rights.

During each of my 16 one-week trips to low-hunter-density states, the many mature bucks I saw chased at will in open areas during peak rut, seemingly with no fear of daytime movements. There were also many mature bucks in each area fiercely competing for breeding rights. On some hunts, I saw as many P&Y bucks in a week as at home in 10 seasons.

An astute observer from a heavily hunted area will notice a sudden decline in mature buck and doe activity and visual sign-posting around the second week of November, indicating the main rut has begun. Another indicator is seeing fawns moving by themselves because their breeding mothers have set them out on their own.

Many gun seasons occur during peak rut, when mature bucks are with or pursuing does, and bucks won't stay within the confines of one bedding area during that entire season. Testosterone levels will occasionally override security instincts, and when bucks are not with hot does, they will transition to other secure areas in search of estrous does, making them extremely vulnerable. The odds of a buck being killed by a gun-hunter off your property are high, so why not take advantage of the situation and plan a couple of strategic bedding area bowhunts before gun season?

SCOUTING AND LOCATION SET UP

Scouting and preparing locations in bedding areas should only be done between the end of the season and spring green-up, which typically starts by May. During the post-season, it's easy to identify rub lines and visual sign from the previous rut, such as scrapes and converging runway hubs.

Ideally, the ground should be bare of snow before you scout. Otherwise, ground scrapes will be covered, and you might inadvertently set up at winter bedding-to-feeding runways, which might be quite different than rut-phase runways. You can identify rut-phase runways when the snow melts.

Several location setups might require multiple days, but during the post-season, bedding area intrusions will have no effect on fall movements. Visual preparation scars — such as runway cleanup, runway alterations, cleared shooting lanes, and entry and exit route trimmings — will become part of the scenery as green-up occurs. Human odor will dissipate, spooked deer will return and deer will resume normal habits well before the season.

Any human activity within bedding areas before the season is a definite no-no. Deer would be spooked after many months of solitude, and the obvious visual alteration scars of new shooting lanes and entry and exit routes would not go unnoticed in the dense foliage. Because summer is a hot, sweaty time of year, you would leave human odor, no matter your scent-free regimen. Any pre-season influx of human activity will alter mature buck activity and make those deer more nocturnal.

After a summer of new growth, the visual sign from the previous rut will be impossible to identify. Pre-season sign would be nothing more than summer bedding-to-feeding-area traffic, which is different than rut traffic.

When your locations are set up, avoid the temptation of placing motion cameras or checking locations for activity, as every intrusion will lower your chances for success and possibly make spooked deer use other bedding areas you can't access. Hunting the interiors of bedding areas in heavy consequential hunting pressure areas is an all-or-nothing proposition. You do it right or don't do it at all.

HUNTING A BUCK'S BEDROOM

You should only hunt bedding areas during the rut phases, and it's advisable to hunt all day. You should commit to being set up and quiet by at least an hour and a half before daybreak and plan to stay until a half-hour after dark. The early arrival should assure that you don't spook deer with entries, and you should leave late, after deer have left. All-day hunts are grueling, but if you do them tactically and in the right types of locations, you might get a kill opportunity at any time of day.

If you have other prime rut locations outside bedding areas, give them the opportunity to produce before hunting bedding area locations just before gun season.

Nearly every state has at least twice as many gun-hunters as bowhunters, and gun-season scouting pressure typically begins a week or so before gun season. The sudden influx of human activity in the surrounding vicinity will negatively affect daytime deer movements and push deer into remote areas, making daytime movements at interior bedding areas more prominent. Deer will continue to chase and breed, but in more secure, secluded and confined bedding areas.

SCENT CONTROL

Because of the typical unpredictable deer movements within bedding areas, coupled with the possibility of rut chasing in all directions, you'll likely have deer downwind of your stand, and a spotless scent-control regimen is a must. Just playing the wind doesn't cut it in bedding areas.

Having hunted for 49 bow seasons, I've tried eliminator sprays and whatever else was available, but until the late 1990s, when I began using Scent Lok's activated carbon clothing, nothing kept me from getting winded.

Proper care and use of an activated carbon-lined jacket, pants, gloves and head cover, used with scent-free knee-high rubber or neoprene boots, have changed the way I hunt, and having deer wind me is no longer a concern.

PARAMETERS

It's wise to only hunt within a bedding area two or three times a year. You might get picked off because there's little foliage cover, might leave a faint scent ribbon on your entry and exit route, or could spook a buck with a hot doe during your entry or exit. No matter the location or hunting practice, the more frequently you hunt it, the lower your odds of success. In other words, don't press your luck by beating it up.

There are exceptions to hunting within bedding areas in heavy consequential hunting pressure areas. If there are several hunters of equal authority at the same property, they might also want to hunt bedding areas. Interiors of bedding areas are not for party hunting but rather for very specific, strategic solo hunting.

CONCLUSION

If your hunting situation allows it, consider a few strategic bedding area hunts during this season's rut. The stigma of hunting a perceived sanctuary might disappear quickly when a mature buck walks into range. ∎

chapter 26

LAST-MINUTE WHITETAILS

NICOLE REEVE

▶ IT HAPPENS TO EVERYBODY AT some point. The early season came and went. October's lull was just that. The pre-rut and rut didn't quite work out. The gun hunters combed the woods weeks ago. Bow hunting season is down to its last couple weeks. Winter is biting. And you have a tag in bad need of a whitetail.

Growing up in southern Illinois, I didn't know what it meant to hunt late-season whitetails. When I came to Minnesota, I learned quickly what real late-season hunting was all about. Nowadays, I often end up with an open tag at home, especially after a busy fall of hunting elsewhere.

Whether your home and hunting grounds are Minnesota, Wisconsin, Canada, the Dakotas, Iowa, New York, Pennsylvania, the New England states — anywhere that snow flies and cold settles in — you have to put together a smart late-season hunting approach.

Late-season whitetail hunting is a detail game. You can't depend on the second rut for reliable action. So hunting becomes a food source scenario. Whitetails will center their lives around the food. It's mostly afternoon and evening hunting, because it's so hard to get into your stand undetected in the mornings.

Center your hunt around good scouting, smart setups and low-impact hunting strategies for the best chance at a late-season buck. But any winter whitetail is a good one.

SCOUT SMART

A late-season hunt begins a couple days before you hit the woods with bow and arrow in hand. (The overall hunting approach I'm outlining also works for muzzle-loader hunters.)

Scout from a distance to find out what fields or feeding areas deer are using. Visibility is good, with foliage down and snow on the ground. You want snow — and

cold — for good late-season hunting.

Park on a back road, field road or ridge and see what the deer are doing without disturbing them. Whitetails get on a pattern. This is probably their most "pattern-able" time of the season, since its earliest days. Study those deer movements and use them to your advantage. Be patient. Figure out what's going on before setting up a hunt.

Pat and I will hunt over a lot of corn and beans. Standing crops are best because the food is usually above the snow. In harvested fields, the deer have to work to get down to any waste grain. But if snow cover is light, stubblefields are good too.

Use scouting cameras in the places you can't watch with binoculars. But avoid checking the units too often and alerting the local deer. Check cameras only every few days. Midday is best. Don't tromp through the woods. Instead, drive up if you can. While you're there, take a quick look for tracks and confirm any well-used trails the deer are using. That's one reason snow is so great.

SETUP STRATEGIES

The best food sources to hunt are away from cover. But whitetails will want to use cover as long as possible on their approach. It might be a point of timber, a brushy or grassy swale, a fenceline, a ditch or creekbottom.

Set up on the travel route to the feed source. You want to be on the approaches where deer will pause before heading out. The ideal hunting situation is to let the does and fawns pass, and have them out in the field when the buck approaches. Seeing them out there will give him confidence. Of course, if you're after venison, shoot that antlerless deer when you can.

Lots of late-season hunting is done on food plots. This can be tough, because food is spread out and deer might come from all angles. If you can control it, put the main food source away from the edge of the timber. For instance, if there's a corn or bean field, leave any standing crops in the middle (not the edge) so the deer have to travel out to it. This is a great way to force the deer to use funnels, pinch points and cover extensions.

Likewise, if you're planting brassicas or other cold season food, don't put them next to woods where the deer can just step out and eat. Put these crops away from the woods so the deer have to use travel funnels to get there.

TREE IT UP OR GET GROUNDED

Hunt out of either a tree stand or a ground blind during the late season. Both have advantages and disadvantages. Trees get you up higher, increase visibility and lift some of your scent above the deer. But they expose you to all the elements, and that makes it hard to sit for several hours. Ground blinds can hide your movements when the woods are bare. Ground blinds also offer some protection from cold winds, and might hold some scent in, but your range of vision decreases.

Set a couple tree stands for different winds. If you can only get one setup, be smart about hunting there only when the wind is right. Your first sit at a spot is usually your best. Wearing whites can help your tree stand chances.

The longer your ground blind sits there, the better. Let the whitetails get used to it for a day or two before you hunt. Brush your blind with natural branches or dried vegetation from the area. For instance, use cornstalks if you're near a cornfield, cattails on the edge of a marsh, or grass in a CRP field.

One beauty of a ground blind is that you can put it where you want it. While a ground blind can control some scent, you still want to wear scent-control garments. With the wind in your favor, a blind around you and ScentBlocker clothes on, you've got "triple" scent protection. That scent-free buffer zone can buy you the time you need on well-educated, late-season whitetails.

APPROACH WITH CARE

One of the hardest parts about late-season hunting, especially in hilly country, is that the deer might be able to see you approach your stand. So we will come in on the truck or ATV, stop with the motor running, get situated, then have someone drive off. The vehicle or ATV usually won't spook deer. Get there early in the afternoon so that if you push some deer off the field or turn some around that were approaching, they have time to settle down and return.

Just as coming in is a challenge without being seen, so is getting out without spooking the deer if they are out in a field or feeding area. It makes me laugh, but sometimes Pat will bark like a dog when we're ready to go. The deer will leave the field, and come back later. It's better to have something "non human" spook them off the feed. Then have a truck or ATV come pick you up.

It takes a dedicated partner to act as driver and pull this off — probably a friend who has his or her tag filled and is willing to help.

GEAR UP FOR COLD CONDITIONS

Drawing a bow when it is cold is not always easy. Nor is getting a smooth release and delivering a quiet, straight-flying arrow.

First, I'll crank down my bow's peak draw weight by 10 or so pounds. It's harder to draw a heavy bow when your muscles are stiff after sitting for two or three hours. Also wear an arm guard so your bow string doesn't catch a sleeve.

Practice shooting in cold conditions. At home or camp, go outside, draw your bow and sling a few arrows before you leave for the afternoon's hunt. This gets the bow's creaks and groans out a little bit — yours too — and gets you "warmed up" to the conditions.

When you get into your stand or blind, draw your bow again, hold it at full draw,

and practice aiming as well. I'll even do this occasionally during the hunt — but only after taking a good look everywhere to make sure no deer are approaching. The more you've rehearsed, the better.

FIND SWEET SUCCESS

Two years ago, Pat and I had hunted our rears off all season in Minnesota. But we just couldn't seal the deal. I was worn out, with hundreds of hours invested. We had even hunted a few late-season mornings, coming oh-so-close.

We had one afternoon remaining. Checking our cameras, we found a field the deer were coming to. Even better, there was a pinch point where they funneled through a downed fence.

We set up early in the afternoon, and 15 minutes before shooting light ended, it happened. The does came out in the field, and then a buck stepped out, just about 40 yards out, and I put an arrow in him. That buck didn't make any record books, but he was a Booner to me after all that effort and hard work.

And that's my final message. Late season is not rocket science hunting, but it is good, old-fashioned hard work. So scout smart. Take care of details. And hunt hard. You can win the winter whitetail challenge. ■

chapter 27

AMERICA'S TOUGHEST RUT ZONES

JOHN WOODS

▶ WHEN TRYING TO ACCURATELY CHARACTERIZE the essence of the Southern rut, one term comes to mind: aberrant. The Southern whitetail rut definitely deviates from the expected course of action.

The rut down South usually — if not always — differs from what is considered normal, or might be described in a textbook on the subject as typical of the species. In the South, the white-tailed deer rut can be anything but typical.

The Southern rut — being highly unpredictable and variable from season to season, state to state and even region to region within individual states — makes hunting big bucks in the South one of the most challenging prospects in the world of hunting. There is no predictable, typical rut — that narrow envelope of time when hunters assume that a buck will momentarily let down its guard in pursuit of does. But Southern deer breed, and they do rut! Timing and intensity are the main bugaboos.

DEALING WITH VARIABLES

Deer hunting season dates vary considerably from Louisiana to South Carolina to Florida and everywhere between. Generally, they run from opening dates as early as mid-August and end in other areas as late as mid-February. Such a wide span of hunting seasons across the vast geography of the South— with differing weather fronts, seasonal temperature ranges, rainfall variations and other factors — makes nailing down any consistent timing of the best hunting dates a huge challenge. It's also a huge source of hunter frustration.

Southern states try to help hunters by posting typical rut phase dates for hunters to focus on, but those dates are hardly set in concrete. Sometimes rutting comes early, other times late and some ruts just trickle in and out. Some seasons, rut behavior never fully materializes in a classic fashion.

So many variables impact the rut that hunters have to rely primarily on actual behaviors they observe as they hunt. These live observations — or ones caught on trail cameras — might be the only confirmation that a rut is in progress.

WILD WEATHER

Weather can prove to be a real nemesis to Southern hunters. In the North, when temperatures plummet and snow or ice arrive, it stays that way until spring. This is far from the case in the South.

In Mississippi, my resident state, weather and temperatures can vary wildly from the bow-season opener in October through the close in mid-February. I have worn short sleeves to the deer stand in December when daytime temperatures exceeded 80 degrees.

The only way to catch deer on the move during these late-season warm spells is at first and last light. Hunters better have a ThermaCELL, too.

A week later, a northern front can blow in with temperatures falling into the upper 30s or low 40s along with 90-percent humidity. Add a northern breeze with a spit of rain, and there's not enough wool in a sheep herd to keep you warm on a deer stand.

Bucks that might have been sweating the week before with no interest in chasing a doe suddenly burst into full rut, apparently stimulated by the cold weather. Hunters have to monitor these changes day by day and be prepared to go hunting at the drop of a hat. Hunting the Southern rut literally means running hot and cold.

Further, nothing can kill a full-bore rut quicker than an unseasonable warming trend. As one friend put it, "When it's 70 degrees, how would you like to be wearing a mink coat chasing your girlfriend around in the woods?"

Most often, rut behavior slacks off quickly as the weather turns warmer.

EATING AND GREETING

Across the five-month deer-hunting season span in the South, wildlife food re-sources can go from lush to scarce. In mast-producing years, oaks will drop tons of energy-rich acorns early in the season. Native browse can be thick and ever-regener-ating when there's ample rainfall. For the most part, Southern deer do not suffer for decent natural foods, except in certain isolated areas or during really tough growing seasons.

As is the rage, supplemental wildlife food plots help fill in the voids. These range from simple crops of rye grass to more advanced agricultural practices involving planting corn, soybeans, winter peas, clovers, brassicas, sugar beets or other exotic crops. These feeds can help carry deer through winter.

Despite these native and supplemental wildlife foods, as the season drags, the resources dwindle — even under the best conditions. The deer populations in the South are so large that the herds are exceeding the carrying capacity in many locales. This narrows the places where deer feed. Thus, deer begin to slowly congregate to areas where food resources exist in a relatively stable supply.

Hunters have to be tuned-in to the available food supplies all season long.

In many parts of the South, a dwindling food supply often begins to coincide with the phases of the rut. Bucks might hit upon a receptive doe found deep in the woods. However, bucks will also begin to troll nearby food sources, searching for does grouped up to feed together.

Deer yards must be located and hunted.

All of these many variables intermingle during the hunting season. The variability of each factor impacts the rutting process at various stages. It is these dynamics at play upon the bucks, the does, and their breeding exchange that makes the South the toughest rut area in America to hunt.

As a result, Southern deer hunters have to adapt with some very demanding strategies and tactics.

HUNTING THE SOUTHERN RUT

Given the variable impact factors controlling the Southern rut, highly successful hunters have to be playing at the top of their game. Two virtues are essential for Southern deer hunters. One is patience. The other is diligence.

"Taking a buck during the South Carolina rut means time in the field is crucial," said Jeffrey Burleson, of Myrtle Beach, S.C. "Mature bucks are taken by logging countless hours in the woods."

It might seem obvious, but hunters cannot collect a trophy from their recliners.

Southern hunters should try every trick in the book. Their hunting style should be highly adaptive.

Many hunters use well-built shooting houses with comforts that encourage prolonged hunts. They also use multiple tree-stand types and sites. They will post ground blinds hidden on the edges of food plots or place portable blinds near active funnels. Some hunters will blind up their ATVs and sit all day.

Southern hunters should also use all the technology available; including scents, sprays, drags and scent dispensers. Cover scents are a great idea. Deer calls should be in every hunting bag and more hunters are dabbling with rattling.

With the crazy ruts we have in the South, it might seem most trophy-class bucks are taken by sheer accident. In most cases though, they are killed through dedicated persistence.

"In Georgia, your best bet is to stay in the woods and you might get lucky," said Hovey Smith, of Sandersville, Ga. "The rut is so unpredictable."

THE MAGNIFICENT 7

The lowest Southern rut intensity is mapped in northwest Arkansas and Louisiana as well as the northern tips of Alabama, Georgia and South Carolina and the southern half of Florida. Generally, the rut intensity is considered moderate across most of Louisiana, Arkansas, Georgia, South Carolina and northern Florida. The highest rut intensity spans from central Mississippi east to the southern two-thirds of Alabama.

Most state wildlife agencies have information on their websites discussing rutting dates across the respective states. Hunters should consult this information for their specific locales.

South Carolina — Oct. 17 through Nov. 13

Florida — Mid-August in southern sectors and mid-November through early February in the panhandle sector

Georgia — Oct. 14 through Jan. 3 with a peak in mid-November

Alabama — Late November to mid-December and can extend from Christmas into February in some sectors

Mississippi — Dec. 6 through Feb. 6 from northern to southern sectors

Arkansas — Nov. 20 through 27; weather impact dependent

Louisiana — Oct. 23 through Feb. 2 from northwest to southeast

WINNING WAYS

Monitoring the known variables is essential and reacting to them quickly is critical. Winning deer hunters pay attention to all the details. They research every trend during the offseason and know the predicted rutting dates where they hunt. They catalog weather patterns and average daytime temperatures. They schedule vacation to coincide with the predicted rut and plan to spend all of it in the deer stand. Yet, they stay flexible.

Being highly flexible and adaptive is paramount. With a weather front approaching, hunt a couple days ahead of it and certainly several days after it passes. Keep monitoring doe feeding areas, travel routes, field corners and funnels. Always react quickly to changing conditions and be ready to hunt, move and hunt more.

"I keep my deer hunting bag packed and ready to go," said Jackson, Miss. trophy hunter Kerry French. "At work, I check the weather for the afternoon, temperature and prevailing winds. If the rut is really on or about to be and the environmental conditions are favorable, I'm out the door."

This attitude is a big part of the winning formula. Southern deer hunters have a lot to contend with when it comes to the rut. Different factors play havoc with the timing of when the rut kicks in and just how intense it might be. It can vary from season to season in every state. Persistent hunters that stay tuned-in to all the critical aspects of the rut as it unfolds and remain ready to hunt at the drop of a hat are the ones who kill the most deer.

Hunting the Southern rut can be tough, but plenty of savvy hunters have learned the right combination to the lock. ■

chapter 28

RUT HUNTING'S 8 BIGGEST MISTAKES

BILL VAZNIS

▶ URP! URP! URP! I STOPPED in mid stride and peered into the ravine below. A mature buck was trailing a hot doe somewhere in the brush-choked cavern. I immediately pulled out a grunt tube and emitted a few long estrous doe bleats followed by a series of tending buck grunts and then waited.

Urp! Urp! Urp! I suddenly realized the buck was heading uphill toward me. I pulled an arrow from my quiver and nocked it just as the 8-pointer appeared to my right. I came to full draw, and the buck stopped behind some brush to look for the source of the bleats and grunts. He nonchalantly dropped his nose to the ground as if to feed, but then snapped his head back up before moving forward in search of the hot doe. When he stepped into an opening, I held my pin behind his left shoulder for a second, relaxed my fingers and sent a razor-tipped arrow into his vitals. The buck ducked and sped off, to no avail. I found him piled up from a double-lung hit less than 75 yards away.

Most of us dream all year about the peak of the rut, when we expect to see wide-racked bucks chasing does with wild abandon at first light or brazenly crossing open fields at noon. Bucks we never knew existed suddenly appear out of nowhere. It should be an easy time to tag the buck of a lifetime, but that's not always true.

There are many reasons for that. Rutting bucks are not as predictable as deer were during the early season and pre-rut periods. They don't behave as we expect them to, and as a result, we commit grievous errors while pursuing them.

Here are eight mistakes to avoid during the breeding season this year.

1. NOT RECOGNIZING THE ONSET OF THE RUT

As the days become shorter, bucks spend more daylight hours searching for estrous does. Most does will soon come into heat, and bucks run crazy to make a connection.

Bucks will cruise the downwind edges of preferred doe and fawn feeding areas, such as cut grain fields, abandoned apple orchards and trails that lead to doe bedding grounds. When bucks hook up with a hot doe, they will stay with her for 24 to 36 hours and breed her before striking out to look for another doe near estrus.

So what does that mean? If you want to see bucks during the breeding season, don't hunt like you did during the early season and pre-rut. For example, one of the hottest pre-rut tree stand tactics is to sit over a primary scrape along a fresh scrape line. However, if bucks are checking out doe feeding areas, doe bedding areas and connecting trails, why would they return to their scrapes? Aside from a few exceptions, they rarely do.

During the rut, it doesn't pay to set up outside a buck's pre-rut or early-season bedding area, because he probably isn't there while he's with does. The same is true for setting up on trails dotted with big rubs. And of course, there's no use trying to ambush a buck near one of his near-dawn or pre-sunset staging areas, either.

You'll realize that when you suddenly stop seeing bucks near their regular haunts during daylight. You'll also notice scrapes and scrape lines are no longer being freshened, and those larger-than-average tracks aren't appearing in buck core areas. You won't see bucks while afield, and you will begin to wonder if they were poached, tagged by another hunter or hit by a car.

So where are they? Out chasing does. That means you must change tactics and begin thinking like a rutting buck.

2. NOT HUNTING THE DOES

If you're a buck hunter, you usually begin the season by avoiding concentrations of does and hunting obscure areas favored by bucks. However, during the rut, it's time to abandon old haunts and seek thickets and feeding areas does find attractive. After all, isn't that what bucks are doing?

If you plan to hunt in the morning, set up near a feeding area used by does and fawns. I like to glass corn lots, alfalfa fields and old orchards from a safe distance at first light. I then hunt the adjacent terrain for bucks until I see does leave for their bedding areas.

You could also still-hunt the perimeter of a feeding area or wait near an exit trail, or set up at a rub line that intersects the doe exit trails at right angles. You would likely only see young bucks if you tried these strategies during the pre-rut, but hunting doe feeding areas during the peak of the rut is a killer tactic.

Another option, especially after a cold front, is to hunt bedding areas preferred by does and fawns. Bucks will weave in and out of these strongholds all day looking for a doe in heat, which makes this tactic a no-brainer — if you can sneak in and out undetected. There is no better magnet for racked deer during the peak of the rut than a bedding area filled with willing does.

3. NOT PACKING A GRUNT TUBE

As the rut heats up, bucks no longer respond to rattling sequences as readily as during the pre-rut. You also can't depend on a response by mimicking a contact grunt from another buck. However, let a mature rutting buck hear a long, drawn-out doe bleat, and he might lower his head and charge your position.

Several calling strategies are best used only during the peak of the breeding season, including buck growling, buck clicking and the snort-wheeze. My favorites involve doubling up one call from a grunt tube with another deer vocalization.

For example, after you emit a doe-in-heat bleat, follow it with a five-second series of staccato-like grunts imitating a yearling buck. That might convince a mature buck that a hot doe is nearby with a younger buck. An older, more mature buck will want to investigate.

If you see a mature doe with a racked buck in tow working just out of range, try a lost fawn bleat to appeal to the doe's maternal instincts. Follow that with a doe-in-heat bleat and a tending buck grunt. That mimics a doe that has abandoned her fawn while being bred.

The biggest buck I ever called in fell for this strategy several seasons ago in Iowa. The 190-class deer was in the middle of a cut cornfield pursuing an estrous doe. I piqued the doe's interest with the fawn bleat, which might have been enough to lure her into range. Still, I quickly followed up with a doe-in-heat bleat and tending buck grunt. As if by magic, the doe moved closer to investigate — with the giant buck sniffing close behind. Unfortunately, she caught my scent 40 yards away and ran off, taking the big buck with her.

4. NOT HUNTING THE MIDDLE OF THE DAY

When the rut is on, the best time to be afield is any time you can get away. Hunting can be exciting at first light, noon or just before dark — and all hours in between.

If you oversleep, and the alarm jolts you out of bed an hour late, don't go back to sleep thinking the day is ruined. You never know when a monster buck will come into view. Even if you only have an hour of free time in the middle of the day, go hunting.